An Indiana Hoosier in Lord Tsugaru's Court

Musings of an American Expatriate Living in Rural Japan

Todd Jay Leonard

iUniverse, Inc.
New York Bloomington

An Indiana Hoosier in Lord Tsugaru's Court
Musings of an American Expatriate living in Japan

iUniverse books may be ordered through booksellers or by contacting:

iUniverse
1663 Liberty Drive
Bloomington, IN 47403
www.iuniverse.com
1-800-Authors (1-800-288-4677)

ISBN: 978-1-4401-2164-7 (pbk)
ISBN: 978-1-4401-2165-4 (ebk)

Library of Congress Control Number: 2009922166

Printed in the United States of America

iUniverse rev. date: 2/25/2009

Dedicated to the memory of

Eriko Chudo Wilkinson;

a mentor, friend and confidant

whom I miss very much…

Contents

Part IV - Political, Educational and Social Issues

Part V - Cultural and Societal Miscellany

Acknowledgements

This book had its genesis in a newspaper column I wrote for *The Shelbyville News*, Shelbyville, Indiana. The content of these articles largely dealt with the everyday life experiences I encountered regularly while living and working in Japan. At the suggestion of more than several regular readers of this column, I set out to rewrite and edit some of the more interesting and provocative essays. The end result is this book.

It is with great pleasure that I publicly thank *The Shelbyville News* for giving me a forum to write about Japan, its people, culture, customs and traditions. The several years that I wrote this column allowed me to put down onto paper my experiences of living and working in Japan over the past twenty years, while at the same time offering the general community a glimpse into a foreign culture and a slice of my life in Japan.

Living half-way around the world, I depended upon a number of people for weekly feedback. I am most appreciative to the editors at *The Shelbyville News*, notably Judy Sprengelmeyer who edited the published weekly versions. I am grateful to all those who sent me e-mailed comments about the articles' contents and to the readership who faithfully read my column.

Conversations with a number of my Japanese friends and colleagues (my "cultural informants") helped me to further develop my ideas and define my thinking while putting this book together. At this time, I wish to thank Mr. Shingo Ono whom I consulted regularly regarding Japanese life, traditions, customs, and language-related topics.

In addition, I wish to acknowledge publicly all those who read parts or all of this manuscript, sparing me from inaccuracies in detail and oversights in assessment. Especially, I extend my thanks to Dr. Frank Takei and Ms. Patti Jill ("P.J.") Stice. They both read the manuscript in its entirety offering valuable insights and suggestions to improve its contents. Of course, while they accept no responsibility for any defects, I am confident their suggestions and candid criticisms have made these essays comparatively better.

To all of these I extend my heartfelt gratitude.

Introduction

There have been so many books written on Japan over the years that there possibly could not be anything new to add to the plethora of literature already out there…or at least one would think so. Historians, sociologists, experts and scholars have written voluminously on Japan, its history, society, people and culture covering just about every aspect of all things Japanese. The dilemma, though, is that Japan—like all cultures—is ever changing and shifting. Like an ocean that ebbs and flows continuously, so does Japanese culture and society. There will always be something new to add to the existing literature on Japan because it will always be metamorphosing, while tenaciously holding on to certain aspects that have endured for eons. Hence, future Japanologists and Japanophiles must not worry that there will come a time when there is nothing new to report or comment upon with regards to this enigmatic and fascinating culture.

This book you are holding in your hands is a compilation of personal observations and experiences that are uniquely my own, so it is impossible that there is any other publication "just like it." Granted, there are certain facets of Japanese culture and society that include customs, traditions and celebrations that are for the most part "matter-of-fact," but these can take on a completely different meaning and significance when interpreted independently through one's own encounters and knowledge based on personal observations and experiences.

This volume is actually a sequel to a previous book, *Letters Home—Musings of an Expatriate Living in Japan* (iUniverse, 2003). Both had their genesis in a column I wrote for my hometown newspaper, *The Shelbyville News*, Shelbyville, Indiana. The original series was called "Letters Home—A Hoosier in Japan" and dealt with my impressions and experiences of living in rural Japan.

The column proved to be a huge hit in my hometown and attracted quite a following. Perhaps the reason why it was so popular amongst the readership was because many people were intrigued by Japan but did not know much about its culture, customs, and traditions. In addition, the writing style—like personal letters—appealed to many people because the articles covered topics related to my everyday-life in Japan, as well as to Japanese history, politics, education, and social issues—but through my eyes and cultural filter. I suppose by reading and learning about Japan by virtue of my perspective, the readers were able to connect personally with what I experienced, which seemed more credible and authentic coming from a person who had the same small-town roots.

All over the United States, as well as in my hometown, Japanese people are a part of the community—some marry Americans and relocate to the US; others come to work in both Japanese and US owned industries; while still others come to study, visit, or just get to know individual Americans through educational programs and sister-city exchanges.

The positive feedback generated from the townspeople, coupled with the success of the first book, I set out to rewrite and edit some of the more amusing and provocative articles which appeared after the first volume's release. The result is this book—a series of letter-essays relating my impressions and experiences of being a foreigner living in rural Japan. The content of each essay consists of information that has been borrowed primarily from my own personal observations and encounters while living in Japan, and from factual information about the various aspects of Japanese society and culture—differing attitudes, customs, and traditions—as I witnessed, experienced, and finally interpreted them.

Therefore, the perceptions and recollections contained herein are my own, so I certainly do not speak for every Westerner living in Japan—nor would I want to as everyone who comes to Japan, and those who eventually choose to call it home, have a different interpretation and reaction to the same situation. These are mine and mine alone.

As a general point of reference, to compare and contrast cross-cultural differences, I do often refer to the United States and my experience being born and raised in the Midwest throughout my essays. This is in no way meant to disenfranchise other Westerners or to give the impression of being "American-centered." Simply, it is what I am and what I know best; it is a compilation of writings about an American teacher from the state of Indiana who lives and works in the countryside of Japan.

The region of Japan where I call home is Tohoku ("northeast" in Japanese), which occupies the entire northern area of the main island of Honshu. This region is made up of six prefectures: Fukushima, Yamagata, Miyagi, Iwate, Akita, and Aomori (located at the very top of the island). Aomori Prefecture (where I live) is further subdivided into three geographical-cultural regions: Shimokita, Nambu and Tsugaru. Each of the three districts has distinct traditions, customs, and even dialects of the Japanese language. The local dialect that is widely spoken on an everyday basis by Aomori natives living in the Tsugaru area is known as *Tsugaru-ben*. The city where I live, Hirosaki, is located in the heart of the Tsugaru region of Aomori Prefecture.

Aomori enjoys four distinct seasons, each with its own charm and allure. Spring, perhaps the most welcome of all the seasons, heralds in the end of the long arduous winter (the Tsugaru region is in the "snow country," with annual snowfall measuring in the meters). Cherry trees are quite abundant in Aomori, so each year hoards of Japanese and foreign visitors from all over the country descend upon Hirosaki to enjoy its world-renowned annual "Cherry Blossom Festival" that occurs at the end of April and beginning of May. Hirosaki Park, the home of the revered castle (which is actually a gatehouse to the original castle structure that is long gone), is awash in pink during the cherry blossom season. The thousands of trees bloom simultaneously, a surreal gift from Mother Nature to all who have the great fortune to behold this majestic paragon of natural beauty.

Map of Aomori Prefecture[1]

The summer season hosts a variety of festivals, most notably the *Nebuta* Festival (in Aomori City) and the *Neputa* Festival (in Hirosaki). During the first week of August, both cities put on spectacular events featuring enormous illuminated paper floats that are pulled through the streets with throngs of people dancing and chanting to beating drums. These festivals occur during *O-bon*, a Buddhist tradition that invites the souls of one's ancestors back to the family home to reunite with living family members. Particularly, this is a family-oriented celebration with families traveling back to their ancestral homes to participate in this observance. These festivals also signal the approaching end of summer, a time when local farmers begin the tedious preparations to harvest their crops. The two main crops in Aomori are rice and apples, of which both are found in abundance.

A *Neputa* Float that is typical of the Hirosaki summer festival by the same name

The autumn season, with its beautifully variegated foliage dotting the mountainsides, is a time of great preparation for the oncoming winter that will arrive all too soon. John Ing, a Methodist missionary from Indiana who came to this area is widely regarded as the "Johnny Appleseed" of Aomori because he was the one who initially brought the apple seeds that were planted here. This unassuming gift started a cottage industry that is now a full-fledged commercial enterprise and staple component of the agricultural landscape. Aomori's climate is perfectly suited to growing apples: a cool climate with little rainfall in the summer makes it a perfect place for apple cultivation. Of course, a variety of harvest festivals take place during this season, most notably the *Kiku Matsuri* or "Chrysanthemum Festival." Life-sized dolls are covered from head to toe with chrysanthemum blooms. As well, this festival features elaborate displays of local agricultural products which showcase the year's harvest.

The winter season in Aomori, which begins early and ends late, is well-known around the country. The snowfall in this area is quite heavy. Several times throughout the season, it is necessary for owners of older homes to hire workers to shovel from the roof the multiple layers of packed snow; not doing so risks a cave-in due to the enormous weight of the snow and ice.

A festival featuring snow lanterns is the highlight of the winter season. Utilizing the tons of available snow, the townspeople shape the snow into lanterns around Hirosaki Park, which are then illuminated at night. The "Lantern Snow Festival" (*Yuki Matsuri*) features a variety of other structures that are sculpted out of snow and ice for the enjoyment of visitors who leisurely stroll through the area wrapped tightly in winter coats and scarves.

Looming majestically over the Tsugaru Plain is Mount Iwaki, known around this area as the "Tsugaru Fuji" because of its conical shape and jutted summit that calls attention to three small peaks. The view of Mount Iwaki from Hirosaki is spectacular. Fortunately, I have an unobstructed view of this natural monument from my bedroom window. The mountain, perhaps, represents the "heart" of the people in this area as it is considered sacred and is revered by the townspeople.

Mount Iwaki's silhouette in early spring

As the four seasons change, so does Mount Iwaki's coat—from the flowering apple trees at its base in the spring, to its lush green blanket of alpine foliage in the summer, followed by its colorful and whimsical coating in the autumn, until finally its white peak in winter proudly extends upwardly showing all its regal symmetry.

The Tsugaru region of Aomori gets its name from Lord Tsugaru Tamenobu who governed this area at the beginning of the 17th century. He built Hirosaki Castle (which was destroyed by fire caused by a lightning strike in 1627) as the symbol of his shogunate. The title for this volume is, of course, a play on words of a well-known work by American humorist, Mark Twain. I thought it appropriate to reference Lord Tsugaru in this way because at times I feel as though I have indeed been transported in a time machine to a different era and place.

An Indiana Hoosier in Lord Tsugaru's Court is divided into five parts. The first section, "Todd's Top Ten List of Things Japanese," introduces ten aspects of Japan that I admire and love. The second portion details "Rites of Passage" in Japan, focusing on the customs and traditions of a variety of life events. The third part describes a number of "Japanese Festivals and Celebrations" which occur with certain regularity, as well as the observances associated with them. The fourth component details current "Political, Educational and Social Issues" facing Japan and its people. And finally, the last section, "Cultural and Societal Miscellany," is a multifarious assortment of topics about various aspects of Japanese culture, society, and daily life.

The year 2009 marks a milestone anniversary for me as an expatriate living in Japan. I first relocated to Japan in July of 1989, and what was intended to be a one year stint has turned into twenty (and counting). Amazingly, this occurred quite effortlessly prompting me to ask myself: "Where did the years go?" It has been an amazing journey, indeed, and one that I cherish deeply. I am quite aware how privileged I am to have been able to live and work in this amazing culture, meeting a variety of wonderful people, and being able to grow on a personal and cultural level. Interestingly, I never planned to live here for so long, it just happened.

In 1989, after finishing a graduate program in history, I was offered an opportunity to live and work in Hirosaki, Japan as an *Assistant Language Teacher* (ALT) on the *Japan Exchange and Teaching (JET) Program(me)*. For two and one-half years I taught English alongside a *Japanese Teacher of English* (JTE) in junior high schools all over the Tsugaru region of Aomori. It was during this tenure as a "one-shot" teacher traveling around the countryside to visit rural schools that I was offered an associate professorship at a local university in the Faculty of Liberal Arts, where I continue to teach today—Cross Cultural Understanding, Comparative Studies, History, and naturally, English.

My first introduction to Japan was as an elementary school child when a Japanese art teacher taught classes at my school. I had heard about Japan from TV programs, magazines, and books (there was a huge "Japan-boom" for some years after the Tokyo Olympics took place in 1964). This teacher, though, really intrigued me. She left her home and family—everything that she knew and was familiar and dear to her—to come to my little town to teach American kids art. Her accent, mannerisms, and style of dress fascinated me.

This fascination continued throughout my life and as a 17-year-old high school student, I finally had an opportunity to experience Japan first-hand. I spent the summer of 1979 as a *Youth for Understanding Exchange* (YFU) student living in a suburb of Tokyo. This experience quite literally changed my life. I had been bitten by the Japan bug and was chronically smitten by its people, culture, traditions, and history. That same summer, the son of the family I stayed with came back to the United States with me and lived with my family for a year. This further cemented my relationship with Japan and by the end of his year in Indiana, my entire family and circle of friends were "Japanophiles."

As an undergraduate student at Purdue University, I settled for studying Japanese history because in the early 1980's few Japanese language programs existed. I did have an opportunity to return to Japan for a summer as a participant on the *34th Japan-America Student Conference* (JASC). After this last trip to Japan, however, I would not return to Japan for a number of years. I did have an opportunity to study at Universidad Complutense in Madrid, Spain, for a year during my junior year abroad. Later, after I finished my graduate work at Purdue, I studied at the Universidad de Costa Rica in San José, Costa Rica as an ambassador of goodwill through *Rotary International's Graduate Scholar Program* as a postgraduate student in history. Each of these places, although unique and interesting, never fully substituted my sincere desire to return to Japan.

Fast forward 20 years. As I embark upon my third decade in Japan, I realize that within just a few years I will have lived half my life in Japan. Little did I know, as I sat in that Japanese art teacher's class as a little boy, how much Japan would become an integral part of my personal and professional life. I, the same as my art teacher, made the decision to leave all that I knew and loved in order to teach Japanese children in a country far away from my roots and home. My yearning for cross-cultural understanding has indeed turned into a lifetime vocation.

Part I:

Todd's Top Ten List of Things Japanese

[1] *Japanese Taxis Clean and Quick!*

When a friend asked me what it is about Japan that I like so much, immediately, a number of things came to mind. As I started to list mentally the aspects I find especially attractive about Japan, I decided to make "Todd's Top Ten List of Things Japanese."

Certainly, high on the list are taxis. In particular, Japanese taxi drivers are clean, quick, and courteous. Often, the drivers wear nicely pressed uniforms, hats, and white gloves. The taxi service that I regularly use instructs its drivers to introduce themselves in the most polite form of Japanese and they nearly always greet me by name.

Competition is quite keen within the taxi industry in Japan so companies do whatever they can to stand out from the others. Some taxi services offer discounts, coupons, or other similar incentives to attract repeat customers. Lately, it has become trendy in my city for companies to offer customers a "user" card where points are accrued each time the taxi service is used. These points can then be exchanged for different prizes or products.

Taxis line up at a train station waiting for customers

One standard feature that all Japanese taxis are equipped with is automatic doors which are opened and shut for the customer remotely by the driver. A lever is used to open the door for the fare to enter, and after arriving at the destination, it is opened again for the passenger to exit. The door is then automatically closed after the customer leaves.

This may seem like a frivolous gesture based on courtesy and politeness, but it has a very practical side to it. Since most Japanese people carry some sort of bag or briefcase, it is quite helpful to have the door opened and closed, allowing the passenger to enter and exit the vehicle without having to juggle items awkwardly or to touch anything that others have touched like door handles.

Once when I visited New York from Japan, I exited the taxi and just walked away. The driver yelled at me to shut the door. It embarrassed me because I had become so accustomed to Japanese taxis that I had forgotten that this is a custom unique to Japan. Also, unlike most New York taxis, Japanese taxis are squeaky clean. The seats are all covered in white seat covers, making it easier to slide in and out. The inside and outside of the taxis are meticulously maintained. Never do I see a taxicab that is banged up, dented, or dirty.

When traveling outside of Japan, I realize how spoiled I am here with the high level of service the customer receives from the taxi companies. Often, American taxis are seemingly on their last legs, with seats so grimy that it makes you wonder what was there before you. Also, drivers are not always the most honest with unsuspecting fares, literally taking them for a "ride." In Japan, since drivers are paid a regular salary that is not dependent upon how many fares they pick up, rarely is a customer driven around aimlessly in order to pad the meter. In fact, it seems that drivers go out of their way to get to the destination as quickly as possible.

On occasion, when a driver has either made a wrong turn, cannot readily find the destination, or has taken a route that ended up in bumper to bumper traffic, he/she will shut the meter off and only ask the customer to pay what would be a fair price for the distance that was expected to be traveled. Now that's integrity.

Another unique trait of Japanese taxis is the type of fuel they use. Nearly all taxis use propane gas instead of gasoline. This custom most likely started as a way to avoid high fuel costs during the energy crisis in the 1970s. I am sure that with the erratic price of oil, which directly affects gasoline prices, it is a bit more economical and energy efficient to use natural gas as a fuel source. Japanese taxis often idle in cues waiting for the next fare, so this clean burning fuel is not nearly as damaging to the atmosphere as fossil fuels.

Japanese people are generally very orderly when waiting in lines of any sort. Train stations nearly always have a taxi stand available for people who need to get to their final destination after taking a train. There is never any pushing, shoving, or cutting in these lines. People very calmly wait as each person in front of them is collected by the next available taxi.

This is certainly not the case in many other countries. On a recent trip to Thailand, I was so frustrated at how some people would cut in line at the taxi stand. These types of people have the attitude of "each man for himself!" Underhandedly trying to hail a taxi several feet in front of another person who has been waiting longer, or grabbing a taxi out from under another person's nose, are examples of poor taxi etiquette. Rarely does this happen in Japan.

Of course, politeness is a well-known Japanese cultural trait, and such behavior would be unseemly, but it is also unnecessary because normally it is so easy to catch a cab. Per capita there seems to be such an abundance of taxis in Japan that hailing one is nearly a statistical certainty. Exceptions would be after a major sporting event where a barrage of people are clamoring to find a taxi or during a rainy season deluge when people are trying to get out of the weather. Nearly always, however, after hardly any time at all, an empty taxi with its telltale illuminated red meter comes cruising down the street.

Taxi fares in Japan do seem pricey to the uninitiated, typically starting at around $6 to $7 for just entering the cab. The total cost of the ride depends upon how far you need to go. The first two kilometers is included in the base price, and then periodically increases around 70-80 cents for each additional 500 meters traveled. It is seemingly based on time as well, because the meter does increase while sitting idly for an extended period. There is also an additional charge of around 20% added to fares from late at night until early morning.

Inebriated passengers who happen to heave the prior festivities out the window and onto the side of the taxi are, of course, charged an additional fee for the cleanup of the taxi. Years ago I heard of a passenger being given a bucket of water to rinse the taxi by a polite driver so the customer would not be charged for the cleanup.

This sums up the professional attitude of the majority of taxi drivers in Japan. They demonstrate a high level of patience (in most instances), and in my experience, display an incredible amount of integrity for their work.

As the customer leaves the taxi, the driver always reminds the person not to forget his/her belongings. However, if an item is mistakenly left in a taxi by a passenger, chances are in the customer's favor of having the item returned.

If I am returning from grocery shopping, the driver always assists me in carrying the bags of groceries into the house. The taxi service I use can have a taxi dispatched to my home in a matter of minutes. I barely get off the phone and put my coat on, when the doorbell rings, announcing the taxi's arrival. Now, that's what I call service!

[2] *No Tipping for Great Service*

Ranking number two on my list of things I like about Japan has to be "tipping"—or the lack thereof. The custom of patrons tipping service related workers in restaurants, hotels, etc. is not normally practiced in Japan—if at all. In fact, service related workers would most likely be insulted if one tried to tip them.

An example of this was when a friend came to visit me from back home. I took her to one of my favorite restaurants where I had become a regular. She was very impressed with our waiter who was especially attentive and friendly throughout our meal. When we prepared to leave, I got up first to pay the bill at the register. As she gathered her things, she noticed I did not leave a "tip" on the table. So to be helpful and to contribute to the meal, she laid down a bill equivalent to about $10.00 in the center of the table before leaving.

A waiter serves *sake* to tourists in a traditional-style Japanese restaurant

We left the restaurant and began walking hurriedly to another place where we had a scheduled appointment. Several minutes later, a very out-of-breath waiter came running after us calling my name. I had no idea why in the world he would be chasing us down because I had double-checked before we left to make sure we had all our bags and coats with us. When he reached us, he extended the 1,000 yen bill to me and said, "You forgot this on the table." I was thoroughly confused because I knew I had not left any money on the table. Since I was speaking in Japanese, my friend had no idea why the money was being returned to me, figuring I had overpaid at the cash register.

I turned to her and said, "How strange…he found this money on our table. I wonder where it came from." She immediately explained that she had left it as a tip, thinking I had forgotten to do so. I then relayed to our waiter that the money was left on the table by my friend, intended for him, because he was so attentive and friendly during our meal. His first reaction was one of puzzlement, which then quickly turned to a look of bewilderment, then embarrassment. To him, it is his job to be friendly and attentive because he is serving us in the capacity as a waiter, and the restaurant pays him a salary to do so. To accept money from a customer would be unethical because it is a part of his job.

My friend tried to force the money on him, but he just bowed graciously apologizing until she took the bill out of his hand. I thanked him for going to the trouble to return the money, and explained that in the United States, it is a custom to leave extra money on the table after a meal as a "tip" to the person who served the food. He admitted he had heard of the custom of tipping, but was still uncomfortable accepting cash from a "regular" customer (such as myself), and especially from a guest (such as my friend) who is a visitor to his country. He most likely felt like it was his responsibility to make sure my tourist-friend received a good impression of Japan, hence his willingness to be so attentive and friendly during our meal.

In Japan, it is often customary for a restaurant owner to offer an added dish as "service" (meaning free of charge) to regular customers. One particular restaurant I have regularly gone to for over 20 years has a core group of diehard customers who prefer to sit at the counter instead of tables in order to chat with the owner as he cooks and serves the food. Often, as a token of appreciation for our continued business, he will make a special dish at the end of the night for all of us to share.

On trips home, I am always perplexed about how much a tip should be, and honestly, I am a bit resentful that I am expected to leave money over and beyond the cost of the meal for service that should be a part of the total dining experience. Before I am inundated with e-mails from waiters, waitresses, hotel workers and the like, I will say that I understand the economy behind tipping as a supplement to the workers' income. However, after living in Japan for so long where tipping is not a custom, I like not having to do it. If the service is indeed poor, is it all right not to leave a tip? I think most Americans feel obligated to leave a tip regardless and, in essence, view it as a part of the total cost of the meal and not solely as an award for good service.

I can think of one instance in Japan when a type of tip is given and accepted willingly. In traditional-style Japanese inns called *ryokan*, it is customary to offer money or a gift as an expression of gratitude to the hotel staff. This custom is called *kokorozuke* and is usually offered at the beginning of the stay. In these types of hotels, the lady of the inn will usually greet the guests at the door, assist them in checking in, and then will accompany them to their room. Once there, she will serve them tea with some sort of snack. She will see to the meals during their stay at the inn, prepare the futons for sleeping, and assist in folding the bedding in the morning. In some Japanese inns today a service charge for this type of individual attention is added automatically to the bill; some of the older, more traditional inns do not. In these instances it is a nice gesture to offer some type of gratuity to the woman. As a high school student, I remember my host mother giving the woman who helped us at our *ryokan* an expensive box of chocolates in lieu of actual cash.

If cash is given, it should be in new bills wrapped in paper or placed in an envelope. It is rude to hand money directly to someone in Japan without first covering it with something opaque. Also, older bills can convey a certain degree of disrespect because it can mean that the person did not take the necessary time to prepare properly the *kokorozuke.* Even shops will place change on a tray as not to offend the customer by handing the money directly. If no tray is available, I have seen shop clerks gingerly hold out the money with one hand, while holding their other hand flat under the other hand like a tray.

Traditionally, if a couple is staying at the inn, it is the woman who gives the money or token of appreciation in the form of a gift as a tip. Historically, dating back to the days of the *samurai*, it was considered beneath a man's dignity to handle money. Still today, many husbands turn over their entire paychecks to their wives, who then handle all household related finances and expenses, doling it out to pay bills, buy food, and even to give back a bit to the husband as his monthly allowance.

Outwardly, it may appear that Japanese husbands are in complete control in the marriage, but do not be fooled by this illusion. The real power lies with the wives because behind the scenes they rule the roosts. After all, Japanese wives have complete charge of not only running the household, the care and education of the children, but also the money. Japanese wives truly do hold the purse strings in Japan.

[3] *The Joys of Public Transportation*

Continuing my series of "Todd's Top Ten List of Things Japanese," I have decided to put "public transportation" in the number three spot. Public transportation in Japan is out of this world. Essentially, one can travel to just about anywhere in Japan using some form of public transportation that is quick, convenient, practical, and always on time. Between trains, planes, buses, ships and bicycles, people travel to and fro all over Japan, every day. I have never owned a car in Japan, and frankly, I do not really need one. I can get everywhere I need to go by public transportation or bicycle.

Even though I only spend a month or two in the United States each year, I do own and maintain a car in Indiana. It is not for luxury, it is out of necessity. I need a vehicle to get to the places I need to go. I did try renting a car on a few trips home, but the cost was so prohibitively expensive that after a few years it became more economical to purchase an older car to have and use when I am stateside. My need is purely functional, so I have a '98 Buick Le Sabre that I drive when I am visiting the US. I use it so little that I figure it will become a classic before I even begin to wear it out.

Since I live at the northernmost tip of the main island of Honshu in Aomori prefecture, getting to and from here can be problematic. When friends happen to be coming to Tokyo on business, they will often e-mail me their itinerary, suggesting we meet for lunch or dinner while they are in town. That would be nice, except it costs me around $500 roundtrip to fly to Tokyo. An overnight bus can get me there and back for about half that, but it takes 9 hours each way. The bullet train is more expensive than the night bus, but still takes a minimum of 6 hours, and costs about $300.

So, unless I am going to be there for another reason that happens to coincide with a friend's visit to Japan, rarely do I make the effort to meet someone for a quick lunch in Tokyo. It would be similar to a Japanese visitor traveling to New York asking a Hoosier in Indiana to meet up for drinks in Manhattan. Of course, I always extend an invitation for people to visit me, but once they realize how much time and effort it takes (not to mention the cost) to travel to Aomori from Tokyo, we usually just have a nice long chat by phone.

That is the primary drawback of the public transportation system in Japan—the cost. For people living here, it becomes a part of daily life, so the cost is not the overriding concern when deciding whether or not to take a trip by plane, bullet train, or overnight bus. It's Japan, of course it's expensive!

With that said, however, Japanese really do know how to make transportation efficient, comfortable, and easy. For instance, when I am needed in Tokyo for business, I will usually fly because the cost is covered by the organization inviting me. For a nominal fee (around $15) I have door to door taxi service that picks me up at my home and delivers me to the airport, which is about an hour's drive. It is called a "jumbo taxi" and it picks up passengers at their homes who reserve a spot ahead of time. This makes traveling to the airport hassle free and easy. Otherwise, I would have to take a regular taxi to the bus station in order to take a public bus to the airport.

From the nearest airport in my prefecture, I take the hour flight to Tokyo. Once in Tokyo, I can hop on the monorail from the domestic airport to central Tokyo where I can take one of many train lines to get to anywhere within Tokyo fast and effortlessly.

In the winter, I rarely chance taking a plane to Tokyo because of the risk that snow will either delay or cancel the flight. Instead, I opt to travel by bullet train (*Shinkansen*) which is quite sleek and comfortable. I especially enjoy the scenery while traveling from the extreme north down to Tokyo in the south. It is quite contrastive to observe how not only the terrain changes, but also the landscape and surroundings, going from a very rural area to ultra-cosmopolitan Tokyo.

Since the *Shinkansen* does not have service to my city, I must take an express train to the eastern side of the prefecture (about two hours away) to catch the bullet train to Tokyo. This means I only have one train change to get all the way to Tokyo, making it quite doable but a bit longer than if I traveled by plane.

The fabled bullet train of Japan is actually made up of a number of separate lines that provide transportation all over the main island, even crossing over to Kyushu Island, terminating in Fukuoka. It glides very smoothly at incredible speeds, passing through cities, towns, villages and farmland as it makes its way to all the major cities.

Passengers may purchase food and drinks from a train hostess on most long distance trains in Japan

A sleeper-train is another possibility allowing passengers to depart in the evening and arrive early the next morning to their destination.

There are a number of options from couchettes, to private rooms, to regular seats on these types of trains. Couchettes are basically a type of bunk bed that allows four people in one compartment. A curtain can be drawn around the bed for privacy. A private cubicle is what I prefer, and is not that much more expensive than the couchette. It is not for people who feel claustrophobic, however, because it is very narrow and only allows you to sit up. A small light and radio is included, as well as a small window to look out. These tiny cubicles remind me of the pods in "capsule hotels" for which Japan is quite well-known.

Private rooms can be reserved as singles or doubles and are priced depending upon the class of service. There are basically two classes: A and B. The "B" class is less expensive and is not as nice. "A" class is nicer but pricier. In addition, there is a "Special A Class" that is quite luxurious, costing around $650 roundtrip per person. It certainly would not be as nice as the Oriental Express, so for the price, it seems a bit exorbitant to spend that kind of money for an overnight train ride. These overnight trains often furnish passengers with a lightweight *yukata* (summer *kimono*) and slippers. For heavy sleepers who do not mind the gentle swaying of a moving train, this mode of transportation is best because it saves one the cost of hotel lodging because the entire night is spent on the train.

Going to Tokyo by bus can be the least expensive, offering a variety of options. Many of my students take a day bus that is quite cheap, but it takes nearly all day to get there. One alternative that I resort to on occasion is the night bus. Leaving at 10:00 pm from my city, it arrives at around 7:00 am the next morning in Tokyo. There is an extra posh "super seat" that I often reserve. It reclines flat, and has a cubbyhole to put your legs, allowing you to lie down completely. It has a curtain that is pulled completely around the seat, allowing for complete privacy.

With a sleep aid, one can get some quality shut-eye, but it is a bus and it does rock back and forth. A toilet is located in the back, but maneuvering the darkened bus full of sleeping people, and using the facilities while it is moving, can be daunting. The restroom is so small that it makes the economy facilities on planes seem big. A hot towel is given to each passenger in the morning to freshen up before disembarking and fighting the infamous Tokyo morning rush-hour on the subway and train lines.

Ships or ferries are other ways to get from the northern part of Japan down to Tokyo, or even further south. These take much longer, but can be fun if time is not an issue.

At the beginning of the essay, I included bicycles. This is not the most practical way to get around Japan if one has to travel a long distance, but many cities do offer bicycles for tourists to either use for free or to rent inexpensively to tour the city leisurely. The city where I live, Hirosaki, has this system and the bicycles can be checked out at the train station and dropped off at a variety of sites around the city.

All in all, I am quite impressed with Japan's innovation and creativity when it comes to public transportation. I can even take a clickity-clackity local train from downtown Hirosaki to my school which takes five minutes (walking takes about 40 minutes). I also have a choice of a bus, taxi, my bicycle, and of course my legs to get me from one place to another.

I am actually glad I do not have a car here because as it stands I have a mere 10 minute walk from my home to my university. I know if I had a car, I would fall into the American habit of driving this short distance. It does force me to stay fit…whether I like it or not.

[4] *Postal and Parcel Services in Japan*

Coming in at number four on "Todd's Top Ten List of Things Japanese" is the amazing postal and parcel service that delivers just about anything to anywhere—all over Japan.

Since Japan is geographically smaller in comparison to the United States, it is much simpler to have an incredibly efficient and effective postal service and delivery system. In recent years, the already superb Japanese postal service has had to step up to the plate, however, in order to keep up with the private companies that can offer better services for less money.

In general, though, the Japanese postal service does a very good job in getting mail delivered in a timely fashion and without any damage. Post offices are found everywhere in Japan making it easy to mail packages, and also to purchase stamps, postcards, etc. Within a two-minute walk from my home is a neighborhood post office which I use several times a week. Another 15 minute walk is yet another postal substation. These are small in size, but are plentiful, making the postal service quite user friendly. Mailboxes are located in many places—even convenience stores—making mailing letters easy and convenient.

Post offices in Japan also have a banking section for savings accounts. In addition to regular banking, I maintain a postal account as well. I appreciate the postal cash machine dispensers because they offer English instructions (both written and oral). Also, when friends visit from home, it is easy for them to get money from their US bank accounts or debit cards using these cash machines. Some regular Japanese banks can be fussy about foreign cash cards, recognizing some systems and not others.

Today, the postal service strives to offer a variety of services geared to making the postal experience easy and more enjoyable for its customers. This was not always the case. When I first came to Japan to live, parcels addressed to foreign destinations could only be mailed from the main post office. Today, all of the postal substations (numbering in the thousands nationwide) can weigh and stamp any parcel going anywhere in the world, making it much more convenient to mail overseas packages.

There are a number of private companies which deliver packages anywhere in Japan, and usually overnight. For instance, frozen or refrigerated goods purchased in Tokyo one day are delivered the next day in a refrigerated truck. Often Japanese will give food as gifts, choosing local delicacies to send to friends and family in other parts of Japan. Since freshness is all important with these types of items, the parcel companies do everything in their power to insure that the items are delivered quickly and in the same condition they were sent.

In Tokyo, there is an American Costco that I like to visit when I have a chance; I usually stock up on a number of things that I normally cannot get so easily where I live. Costco will pack all of the goods I purchase in boxes and mail them to my home via one of these companies—and all for a very reasonable amount of money. The reason it is so inexpensive to mail boxes around Japan probably has to do with the sheer volume of parcels that are sent each and every day. Also, competition between companies is very keen as it is a very lucrative industry. The best way to stay ahead of a rival company is to be more efficient, cheaper, and careful with the entrusted cargo.

I especially appreciate the private delivery companies' attention to detail. They handle each package with extreme care. Never in all the years of utilizing such services have I ever had anything broken, lost, or misdirected. I cannot say this about the US Postal Service.

In Japan, they have created nearly a foolproof system that tracks each package individually. When mailed, the package is given a regional code, then a more specific code that takes it to the street where it will be delivered. Also, these delivery services regularly pick up packages from a variety of places—convenience stores, department stores, supermarkets, liquor stores, drycleaners, and even from one's home.

One service they provide that I particularly like is a suitcase delivery system. Before leaving on an international trip, I can mail my suitcases from my home to the airport I am leaving from for about $10-$15 each. This really makes traveling hassle-free because getting the luggage to Tokyo using public transportation can be the most difficult part of a trip and the most frustrating. By having the suitcases arrive before, all that needs to be done is pick them up and check in.

Returning to Japan is the same. Located outside of customs at all international airports are several counters for people to send their luggage back to their homes. Nearly all people who live outside of the Tokyo-metropolitan area utilize this service. Trying to lug heavy suitcases up and down stairs, through busy train stations, and onto buses is too much for even the heartiest of travelers. The Japanese system of mailing luggage to and from the airport makes it all that much easier.

This system of parcel delivery has certainly spoiled me over the years. I had a severe case of sticker shock when I tried to mail a small suitcase from Minnesota to Indiana once using an American parcel service. There are few bargains in Japan, but mailing boxes and parcels around the country happens to be one of them.

[5] *State of the Art Toilets in Japan Flushes Ahead*

Coming in at number five on the list is a topic that is near and dear to my heart: Japanese toilets. The Japanese have not only perfected the basic design of the hardware used in these items—they have magnificently transformed the mundane need for daily elimination into a surreal experience that make visitors to this country swoon with contentment.

A case in point: In 2005, Madonna returned to Japan for a concert after a nearly 12-year absence. When she met with entertainment reporters at a press conference, she commented to the packed room that she had missed terribly Japan's warm toilet seats. This remark caused the attendees to chuckle, knowing exactly what she meant.

Living in a cold climate (as I do here) makes having an electric toilet seat that stays warm a necessity and not a mere indulgence. For people who take for granted central heating, it may seem like a superfluous extravagance to have a heated toilet seat. However, to those of us without the luxury of central heating, it is indeed a welcome salutation first thing in the morning upon waking up from a night's sleep. Being greeted with a toasty-warm toilet seat rather than a burst of icy-cold plastic on one's derriere is much appreciated. Trust me.

For instance, a standard feature on Japanese toilets is a sink that is built into the design of the lid on the toilet tank. Instead of having a separate sink to wash one's hands after using the facilities, a small basin and faucet can be found on most Japanese toilets. When it is flushed, the clean water washes the person's hands, filling the tank, which will then be used by the next person to flush the waste away.

A Japanese Western-style toilet equipped with a basin to wash one's hands

This is an ingenious design, saving water and making the toilet multi-functional. A towel rack is often positioned to the side of the toilet, in order for the users to dry their hands after rinsing them in the water that fills the tank.

Recently, a friend from Australia came to visit me here and was especially impressed with this feature of the toilet…as well as the heated toilet seat. She made a point to photograph the toilet in my home to show her husband, commenting that it was such an efficient use of water. I have to agree with her. It is more environmentally sound, and makes perfect sense to have a double-use for the water that will eventually be flushed away.

Most toilets in Japanese homes are in separate rooms, away from the bathtub and sink used for bathing and washing one's face and brushing one's teeth. A small room called a *senmenjo* (which usually doubles as a laundry room with a washing machine) is where people wash their face, hands, and brush their teeth. Next to this washbasin room is the *ofuro* or bathroom.

When I first visited Japan in the late 1970s, it was common to see the letters "W.C." on all lavatory doors to toilets. This acronym was borrowed from Great Britain, short for "water closet," which labeled the toilet room. The W.C. is considered by Japanese to be much too dirty to be combined with washing and grooming oneself, so it is nearly always separate. The one exception is in many efficiency apartments which utilize a "unit bath"—an entire bathroom including toilet, sink and tub in pre-molded pieces. Also, Western-style hotel rooms often have all-in-one bathrooms.

Having lived in Japan for so long, though, I have to say that I like having the commode completely separate from the bath and sink-basin. It just makes hygienic-sense to keep the two functions isolated from one another. Studies have shown that anytime a toilet is flushed, it sends small particles of waste from the flushed water out into the air. If toothbrushes, towels, soap, and a bathtub are in the same room, these items get covered in this sullied mist. I have noticed that some new homes in the United States are beginning to separate the two areas of the bathroom by isolating the toilet in its own little room. A welcome change in house design, for sure.

Japanese are so finicky about cross-contamination from the toilet that special slippers are even provided for guests to use while in the toilet. These are usually plastic, making them easy to clean, and are only worn in the toilet room. These slippers will sometimes have the letters "W.C." on them, so if someone forgets to take off the "toilet" slippers after using the facilities, everyone will know. An embarrassing situation indeed, especially at a dinner party, when the host has to point out to a guest that he/she forgot to change back into the regular house slippers after using the toilet.

The current rage in Japan is the "washlet" or bidet-style toilet. These are very high-tech and are now being placed in public restrooms all over Japan in department stores, office buildings, and restaurants. Most homes built in the last decade or so have as a standard feature this function on the family toilet.

These are nothing new, first introduced to Japan in 1964 by—believe it or not—an American company. However, after just two years on the Japanese market, the "Wash Air Seat" went into domestic production and the rest is history. Virtually unheard of in the United States today, these types of toilets are now standard features here. And how they have evolved over the past 45 years!

An American friend who has lived in Thailand for thirty years came to visit me last December. We were touring Tokyo and staying at a very reasonably priced hotel. Even this modest hotel had installed in each room one of the fancier models of these bidet-style toilets. My friend was so impressed with all the bells and whistles included on his hotel room toilet—heated seat, temperature and pressure controlled water for the derriere and a separate mode for women to use—he jokingly said he could forgo seeing Tokyo in order to stay in his room to enjoy the toilet. He was determined to get these "washlet" toilets installed in his home in Bangkok.

His reaction is typical for the uninitiated. Japanese bidet-toilets are certainly spoiling, and once a person has experienced one of these new-fangled contraptions, ordinary toilets just seem, well, humdrum. However, this type of luxury comes at a hefty price. This is no deterrent to Japanese people who gladly fork out the money to have these installed in their homes. Just like some Americans who think they cannot live without a refrigerator with a water dispenser and icemaker on the door, automatic dishwasher, or garbage disposal in the kitchen, Japanese people feel the same way about their "washlet" toilets. Rarely do Japanese kitchens have any of the amenities just mentioned that are typically found in American kitchens, but the majority of toilets in Japan are "washlets."

Home builders regularly, as a matter of course, include an additional hookup for water for these in new bathrooms, and an electrical socket can be found behind all toilets to plug in the heated seat. Some of the swankier models come with a remote so the user does not have to twist around to fumble with all the buttons found on the side of the toilet seat.

I know that a stratum of American society would embrace this technology in a New York minute—if the price would come down. Few Americans want to pay $800-$1,000 for a toilet seat. Interestingly, luxury options when purchasing a car is something that most Americans do not flinch at when choosing comfort and style over pure function.

Why not let this attitude extend to the one place where people do spend a goodly amount of time on a daily basis? It is well worth the high price, and once you try one of these high-tech toilets, you will never be satisfied with the common, run-of-the-mill toilet ever again.

[6] *The Japanese Bath (a.k.a. Heaven on Earth)*

Continuing on with my series of favorite things about Japan, number six on the list is the *ofuro* or Japanese bath. There are few things in life as satisfying and luxurious as a traditional Japanese bath. Over the millennia, Japan and its people have truly perfected bath-taking—elevating a mundane process of daily hygiene into a veritable art form, one that is steeped in ritual and, in my opinion, could be regarded as a precious and treasured cultural asset of Japan.

Many first-time visitors to Japan are a tad apprehensive about two aspects of taking a Japanese bath: 1) entering bath water that has been used by someone else; and 2) bathing with strangers in communal or public baths.

Admittedly, on my first visit to Japan as a 17-year-old high school exchange student I, too, was not very keen about baring it all with a group of strangers, or getting in a tub after several people had already used it. However, after just one time, I was hooked. All apprehensions were cast aside, and I am now a big fan of all types of traditional Japanese baths: the home bath, communal or public bath, and the hot spring baths (known as *onsen* in Japanese).

It is necessary to keep in mind that the Japanese bathtub is not used in the same way people use a bathtub in most other countries. The Japanese bathtub is used only for soaking and not washing. The water is clean and steamy hot—so blistering sometimes that it seems like it is going to scald your skin. So, in reality, one is not really bathing in the true sense of the word, meaning splashing about in soapy, dirty water as is the custom in the West. The Japanese bathtub is used only for

A typical-style Japanese "home" bath

soaking and relaxing, similar to a hot tub's intended use, except without swimming trunks and massaging bubbles.

I tend to be much more apprehensive about getting into a hot tub than I am about entering a Japanese bath because before entering the actual bathtub, proper Japanese etiquette obliges the bather to first thoroughly soap, scrub, and rinse off their bodies before setting foot into the hot water. Most people enter a hot tub without bathing, knowing that so much chlorine is in the water that, like a pool, a shower afterward is needed.

From early childhood, Japanese children are exposed to traditional Japanese baths and learn early on how properly to wash their bodies. In Japanese families, children's bath time is nearly always done with Dad. From the time the children are babies, Dad is the one who usually bathes with the children giving Mom a short break after dinner. Most every adult Japanese person can pull out a photo with Dad in the bathtub, usually as a small baby, taken by Mom. This custom of children bathing with Dad continues until they reach an age when they can bathe alone. As a family outing, many Japanese families will visit a public or natural hot spring bath on the weekend. Some newer and more modern public bath facilities offer a "family bathroom" where an entire family can bathe together in privacy—mother, father, and children.

Quite numerous in the old days, mixed public baths (that allowed both men and women to bathe together) are not so common today. The Christian missionaries who came to Japan in the late 1800s tried very hard to nix this custom, and eventually were largely successful except for traditional *onsen* that often feature several outdoor baths called *rotenburo*. A number of these allow both men and women to bathe together still today.

When friends visit from home, I like to take them to my favorite traditional-style *onsen* in the mountains that offers a variety of baths, including a communal outdoor bath that is mixed. This particular bathhouse is actually a traditional Japanese inn. It is located so far away from civilization that it has no electricity. Cell phones are unable to pick up any signal. For travelers wanting to truly get away from it all, this is the place to go for total relaxation away from the clutches of modern technology. At night, oil lanterns are lit all around the inn and the surrounding grounds, giving it a magical and surreal appearance.

In the summer, guests scurry from bath to bath in their cotton *yukattas* (summer *kimono*) enjoying all the various baths, each boasting different health benefits. The mineral water in these baths is well-known around the country for its medicinal value that helps relieve chronic conditions such as arthritis. The bathers first bathe inside with soap to clean their skin before going outside to try out all of the different baths located around the inn.

In the winter, the only way to access this inn is by snowmobile. Upon arrival, special winter *kimonos* are offered to guests; these are thicker, giving people a semblance of warmth as they go from bath to bath. Guests learn to disrobe quickly in the cold weather, plopping themselves down in the immediate warmth of the outside baths. It is indeed serene to sit quietly, enjoying the winter snow falling gently upon your head.

Japanese, as a people, are very modest, so a small towel is used to cover the important parts as one enters and exits the bath. There are partition-less stations all around the periphery of the bathroom equipped with a small wall mirror that each person uses while bathing. Bathers sit on small stools, low to the ground, utilizing a small wash pan for rinsing the soap off their bodies. Even though the next person is only inches away, one has a feeling of being alone.

Really self- or body-conscious people may find a Japanese public bathing experience to be much too torturous to bear; but in fact, it is such a common and natural part of Japanese people's lives, that no one pays other bathers much attention. Perhaps by sitting low to the ground, and in front of this small mirror, psychologically it gives one a sense of privacy. After all, it would be rude to stare and besides, everyone is in their birthday suits, so what's the big deal?

For the shy and uninitiated, perhaps the privacy of a home bath would be best to try first before bathing in a communal bath. Home baths are typically wide and deep, allowing bathers to submerge up to their necks. The most wonderful part about a Japanese bathroom is that bathers do not have to be careful about splashing water about because the entire room is water-resistant. The walls, ceiling and floor can be sprayed with water without worry. Also, the shower nozzle is not attached to the wall—it is on a detachable hose used to rinse your body and hair while sitting or standing. This also makes cleaning the bath quite easy. Little, plastic boots are sold at supermarkets that can be worn while scrubbing down the bathroom.

In fact, there are a number of interesting bath-related accessories that people buy for the bath. A cover is used between bathers to keep the water hot; and in the winter, it helps to hold the heat in the bathtub while the person is bathing because the typical bathroom is unheated. A stir-stick is used for non-temperature controlled baths to make sure the hot water is evenly distributed. A bucket and stool, as well as a smaller ladle-like container are used for the actual body-washing portion of the bath. A long and narrow washcloth is used for scrubbing the skin. Its rough texture reminds me of sandpaper, and basically has the same effect.

Generally, Japanese people have beautiful skin, often resembling silk. I believe this has a lot to do with the bath ritual they perform daily. I am always amazed at how thorough people are, even children, when bathing at a public bath. Children scrub and scrub their little bodies with such determination, learning by observing and mimicking their parents. These rough washcloths exfoliate, sloughing off dead skin cells from the body. This keeps the skin smooth and silky. Since many Westerners opt for a morning shower, forgoing the use of any type of washcloth, they are only washing off the dirt and grime for the most part, and not all of the dead skin cells.

I still insist upon a morning shower because this is a part of my culture. In addition, though, I relish taking a luxurious and relaxing Japanese bath before bed—the best of both worlds.

[7] *There's No Splitting Hairs when it Comes to Japanese Hair Salons*

Continuing on my list of "Todd's Top Ten Things Japanese" is number seven, which is actually a composite of several things I like. All, however, are related to getting one's hair cut in a Japanese salon.

The city where I live has a disproportionately high number, per capita, of hair salons and barbershops. This fact rarely goes unnoticed by Japanese and foreigners alike who visit my city. Just about every corner, and certainly on nearly every street, there is a beauty shop, hair salon, or barbershop. I do not really think people's hair grows faster here than in other places, or that they have more of it, necessarily, but for some quirky reason, we are inundated with hair salons.

Over the years, my hair has gone from being so bushy it was unmanageable, to being quite thin on top...but no matter, I still treat myself at least once a month to an afternoon at the hair salon—hair or no hair. Perhaps the biggest difference that sets Japanese hair salons apart from their American counterparts is the attention to the minutest of details to ensure that the customer has a pleasurable and enjoyable experience.

After all, competition is keen and getting the city's finite number of potential customers through the door is certainly a case of "survival of the fittest." Just as new salons open on a weekly basis, a number of established salons close their doors. Offering extra services, and going the extra mile to make sure the customer is satisfied, is a reality of the hair-design industry in Japan.

Being pampered is a part of the Japanese hair salon experience. Members of the salon staff—from the door greeter, to the shampooer, to the cutter, to the receptionist—all go out of their way to make you as comfortable as possible.

For instance, when one gets a haircut in Japan, the shampoo-person places a sheer cloth over the client's face to protect the eyes from any wayward soap suds that may inadvertently fly around. At least this is the reason I am always given by Japanese people regarding the face veil, but I tend to think it has more to do with modesty and discreetness in order to offer the customer more privacy. Being in such close proximity with the shampooer, face to face, could make the client uncomfortable. So, the simple solution is to cover the person's face in order to avoid any awkwardness and eye contact. Perhaps this is another reason why the face is covered—so the client and shampooer do not feel obligated to engage one another in conversation.

There is not a lot of chit-chat during this process except for a couple of predetermined questions the shampooer asks the client: "Is the water temperature all right?" and "Does your head itch anywhere?" Of course, the standard responses are "Yes, the water is fine." and "No, my head doesn't itch anywhere."

Many years ago a television program placed a hidden camera at the shampoo sink of a busy salon. Even though all the clients said their heads were not itchy, as soon as the shampooer was finished, each person reached up to scratch a part of their head. Perhaps it would be too assertive to instruct the shampooer to scratch the head, even though he/she offered to do so. Humility is the key, and being a bother to another—even a service-related worker—is not being humble.

However, it is during the shampooing part of the process that the client is the most relaxed; the forced quietness is refreshing, allowing the customer to be transported to another place. It is meditative to have the head massaged for 5-10 minutes by the shampooer, using a variety of aromatic hair products in the process.

It is a cultural trait of Americans to pass time with banalities that often times have no purpose or real meaning. We are uncomfortable with prolonged silence. In Japan, silence is not necessarily an indication of boredom or anger or any other underlying reason other than it is sometimes peaceful to be alone with your thoughts. It is all right to have nothing to say. I have learned to relish this aspect of Japanese culture, enjoying a long car ride through the mountains without feeling the necessity to fill the entire time up with inane conversation.

The shop I patronize offers customers hot tea or coffee in the winter, and a cold barley tea or ice coffee in the summer. Of course, the cups are dainty and elegant, with the latest magazines neatly laid out at the station where the hairstyling is done, along with the selected drink. To protect the client's clothes from hair clippings and chemicals (like hair dye or permanent solution), some shops offer customers a light *kimono*-wrap to wear over their street clothes to keep everything pristine. Once finished the entire staff walks customers to the door, bowing and thanking them for their business. Of course, such individual attention is not exactly cheap, but not outrageous either.

The same thing is true for barbershops featuring the tell-tale red, white and blue swirling striped poles. One of my most favorite things to do here, and something I've never had done in the United States, is to get a shave.

In preparation for the shave, the barber places steaming hot towels all around the face area to open the pores. Then, hot lather is generously put all over the face. A straight razor is then used to shave the face. In Japan, everything on the face gets shaved—forehead, nose, and even the tops of the ears. In fact, one of the most relaxing things to have done at a barbershop while getting a shave is to have your ears cleaned.

The barber uses a small scoop-like instrument to scrape gently away all the little hairs that grow around the earlobe and in the ear canal. Admittedly, the first time I had this done, it was a bit nerve-racking to have a stranger put long metal instruments deep into my ear canal. It goes against all conventional wisdom given to me as a child that nothing smaller than your elbow should ever go into your ear. Luckily, these people are highly trained and are very careful when probing around in the ear.

Japanese wives, as a way to show love for their husbands, will gladly do this little chore. The husband lies with his head in her lap, submitting completely as a way to show his absolute trust in his wife. Japanese children lay with their heads in their mothers' laps, as well, to have their ears cleaned.

It is a pleasurable experience, once you relax and the initial fear of having someone poking about your ear with what looks like medical instruments dissipates. It is an experience that I welcome and appreciate.

A new type of hair salon and barbershop has started to become trendy—the discount cut with no frills. In these shops, the customer buys a ticket out of a vending machine and waits in the order he/she arrived. The stylist wets the hair with a squirt bottle and does a very standard haircut with no shampooing, massaging, beverage, or other perks normally associated with hair salons in Japan. The normal 60 to 90-minute hair session of full-service salons is whittled away to a mere 15 minutes or so in these new types of conveyer belt establishments.

These "in and out" shops, at first, catered largely to students on a budget and salary men who had no time for the lengthy full-service treatment. Today, men and women both patronize these establishments because people are more "yen" conscious than in years past when it comes to seeking out discounts and bargains.

A dear friend of mine here wanted my mother to experience a Japanese hair salon, so as a gift, she treated my mother to a full-service treatment—head and back massage, shampoo and conditioning treatment, and a stylish Japanese-style haircut. My mother loved the experience and was very appreciative to have had the opportunity to be pampered with the royal hair salon treatment. The close-cropped haircut, at first sight, did surprise my stepfather who was accustomed to her normal hairdo, but he soon got used to the new look.

If ever you find yourself traveling to Japan, forego getting coiffed before your trip and wait until you are here to have a unique hair-experience. You won't regret it. I promise.

[8] *The Fine Art of Gift-Giving in Japan*

Number eight on my "Top Ten List" of things I like about Japan is the custom of "gift-giving." I am sure all cultures, everywhere, perform a similar time-honored gift-giving ritual, but there is something institutional about the way Japanese give and accept gifts, making it an engrained and essential component of their rich and vibrant culture.

Officially, there are two times a year that Japanese give gifts—*chugen* in midsummer and *seibo* at the end of the year. Stores put up elaborate displays during these two seasons in an effort to lure customers into buying the exquisitely wrapped packages. Often, however, these gifts are not given without some strings attached, meaning there is sometimes a strategic reason for giving a gift of a certain value to a particular person. Perhaps the receiver of the gift had assisted the giver prior to the gift-giving season and hence feels an obligation to repay that assistance with a gift; or perhaps the gift-giver is anticipating the need to ask a future favor of the receiver, and an expensive summer or year-end gift will help ease the burden of asking for that assistance. In either case, the gift can be a sort of bargaining chip with the other person.

This is not to say that these types of gifts are not ever given just for the sake of giving, because in most instances they are offered without any future expectation or ulterior motive. Japanese people, in general, are a wonderfully generous group of people making gift-giving a natural part of their cultural-being. Gifts here are sometimes used to cancel out obligations to others as well. For instance, if you do me a favor, and I reward you immediately with a "thank you" gift, then I have effectively neutralized the obligation I may have to you for the favor you did for me.

Once when I had a group of students to my home for a barbecue, we wanted to take a group picture. Since everyone wanted to be in the photo, we needed someone to take it. Since my neighbor was working in the yard, he was the logical solution to our dilemma. Happily he came over to take our picture, and I, of course, thanked him for doing this. As he was exiting the backyard, one of my female students very naturally, and without consciously thinking about it, reached down to the table and picked up an unopened package of cookies that she then elegantly, and quite effortlessly, offered to him as he departed.

I thought at the time, "Boy, she's smooth." The whole transaction occurred in one well-ordered glide of her hand, thus canceling out any obligation we may have had to him for doing us this favor. It was a natural, cultural reaction for her to do this. In the United States, a simple "thank you" would have sufficed, and no one would have felt the need to give anything further to the person for doing something as mundane as snapping a photo.

On another occasion, I was surprised by a neighbor who lived one street over. He and his daughter showed up at my door bearing a gift-basket of beautiful homegrown apples in pristine condition. I was not so familiar with this neighbor and, in fact, he had to explain to me where exactly his house was located. Also, he admitted to me that we had never actually met in person, but we had greeted one another on the street from time to time.

One disadvantage of being a foreigner in rural Japan is that we stand out so much that everyone knows who we are, but often we have no idea who everyone else is. In this case, however, I was at least marginally familiar with him, but his sudden generosity made me a bit uncomfortable and somewhat suspicious of his motives. Why, I kept wondering, did he go to all the trouble to visit me—out of the blue—and why did he make a point of bringing his daughter along?

It only took two days to learn the answers to these questions, and in turn, his motives for the rather unexpected (and certainly abrupt) act of previous generosity: He was hoping that I would agree to tutor his daughter in English. She was preparing to take the entrance exam into high school and needed supplementary lessons to get her up to snuff. Mystery solved.

Fortunately for me, and unfortunately for her, I was going abroad during the time she needed the lessons, thus relieving me of any obligation. Be that as it may, I still felt a hint of indebtedness to this neighbor for the gift of apples I had received before. Quick thinking on my part, I remembered I had a bag of *kaki* (Japanese persimmons) which had been given to me a day or so before by a student. Excusing myself momentarily, I gathered an assortment of these fruits and offered them to my neighbor. Thus, effectively canceling out any obligation I may have had—in kind—to him and his daughter.

The "recycling" of gifts is commonly practiced in Japan—as long as they are in their original, unopened packages, or in the case of fruits and vegetables, fresh and in impeccable condition. Not being a huge fan of persimmons, however, I was happy to not only cancel out my prior obligation, but to also unload something that likely would have gone to waste—a win-win situation.

When invited to someone's home in Japan, it is customary to arrive with some sort of gift-offering. It can be a small bunch of cut flowers, an assortment of fruits or cakes for dessert, or a bottle of wine—just about anything. Again, this offering helps to cancel out any obligation that may have been incurred by "imposing" upon the host.

This particular gift-giving custom is now so firmly a part of my cultural-being that whenever I am invited to someone's home for a meal or coffee, whether in Japan or elsewhere, I feel it necessary to contribute some sort of offering as a "thank you" gift to the host. It is such a nice custom. Hosts certainly do not expect gifts from guests, but appreciate the gesture all the same. After so many years of cultural conditioning in Japan, I feel naked arriving to someone's home for dinner without some type of appreciation gift in hand.

I have acculturated so much to this custom that I even feel the need to bring some sort of souvenir or gift from Japan to family and friends back home. I feel odd arriving back to Indiana without something to give the people I meet. The problem is I have exhausted all of the possible options, having given just about every type of Japanese trinket and bauble imaginable.

The Japanese have certainly perfected the art of gift-giving into a national virtue. From small Mom & Pop shops to huge department stores, nearly all of these enterprises offer "gift-wrapping" as a matter of course (and free-of-charge) to all their customers. One cannot swing a *samurai* sword here and not hit a place that has ready-made gifts for the picking. Every train station, airport, and tourist attraction—as well as a myriad of other public places—has counters where *omiyage* (souvenir gifts) can be purchased. Businesspeople who must travel away from their office on an official trip nearly always return with some sort of *omiyage* in the form of food for the entire office to enjoy. It is expected by the person's colleagues, and is a firmly rooted custom in Japanese business culture. These gifts come in a variety of sizes (depending on how many people are in the office) and each cake or cookie is individually wrapped for easy distribution.

One valuable lesson I have learned whilst residing in Japan is never to look a gift-horse in the mouth. I graciously accept whatever is offered—even if it is something I may not need or even want. After all, I can always recycle it.

[9] *Attention to Details...Truly a Japanese Quality*

Nearing the end of my "Top Ten List of Things Japanese" is number nine. This is not one singular thing, but various things that I am going to classify into one category: "attention to details." When foreign guests visit me in Japan, this is one of the first things they notice about Japan and the Japanese—a wonderful respect for the finer points and niceties that help to make daily life that much more pleasant.

Whether it is the nicely uniformed janitorial workers at train stations; or the hot towels customers are offered when entering many restaurants and coffee shops (to refresh their faces and wipe their hands); or the way women gingerly tuck under and fold into a triangular shape the top layer of toilet paper on the roll after using it (to make it more attractive for the next person who reaches for it), Japan is a detailed-oriented country. I could go on and on, because there are so many little things that are done regularly in Japan to make whatever experience you are having just that much nicer. Politeness is a well-known trademark of the Japanese, which transfers to all facets of society and daily life.

In fact, most of the attention to details I find so intriguing here are rooted in this pervasive sense of politeness as an attempt to make the occasion or situation more comfortable and convenient for others. Now that I am clearly middle-aged, I am amused at some attention to details that are designed to make life simpler and easier for those of us who are getting older. In public spaces (like post offices, government offices, hospitals, and banks) items are offered for the aged to utilize while transacting their business. These additional efforts to make a mundane experience more refined show the level of respect that older people in Japan are afforded.

For instance, in many of these establishments, displayed prominently is a selection of prescription eyewear to borrow while conducting the business at hand—in case people either forgot to bring their own or are too vain to wear glasses in public. Normally, there are three types that come in bright red, yellow, and blue frames. Each one is distinctly marked with the intended age of the user: For people in their "40s," "50s" and "60s and older."

Although the prescription is not exact for every person that falls within the prescribed age group, it is approximated to the average eyesight of a person around that age. In a pinch, the eyeglasses will suffice momentarily to read the fine print on a document or to see to sign one's name. Fortunately, I have never had to resort to using these as I wear my own glasses all the time. I do see customers frequently reaching for these to use when trying to conduct business, reading small print, or when filling out a form.

For some reason, eyeglass stores in Japan are very plentiful. In my city alone, I bet there are over 100 shops specializing in eyewear. One attention to detail that these shops offer to the general public is an electronic cleaning machine that passersby use to clean their eyeglasses while on the run. Outside many of these stores, a table is set up with a sonic-vibrating contraption that uses liquid to clean the lenses and frames completely. Tissues are provided to dry the glasses, as well as an adjustable mirror to make sure they are on straight.

Speaking of mirrors, many public places in Japan display mirrors with small advertising on the edges for people to primp and peer at themselves when passing by. This attention to detail serves two purposes: it is a free service for the general public, while allowing a company to advertise to those people who stop to use it.

Another form of advertising that many companies employ is to place staff outside train and bus stations to pass out packs of tissue. It is rather easy for a passerby immediately to throw away a mere piece of paper, but something as useful as tissue is more likely to be placed in a bag or pocket for later. Each time it is used, the advertisement is noticed.

This is a very clever way to advertise and an attention to detail that is greatly appreciated by people who suddenly find they need tissue...and fast. In many public spaces, toilets are readily easy to find, but often these do not provide toilet paper. Usually tissue vending machines are provided so one can purchase a package of tissue in an emergency. However, most people tend to carry the free tissue packets handed to them on the street. This makes it all the more likely that someone given a tissue package will eventually use it.

Actually, a number of service-oriented businesses regularly use a form of advertising that involves a free gift that is useful or needed by the consumer. In the summer, some companies pass out hand-fans to commuters in the heat of the day. Again, it is something practical that helps to alleviate the heat, so the person will keep it for another occasion. I suppose this is not so different from an American real estate office passing out refrigerator magnets with all the necessary contact information included, or an insurance company that offers pens with the company logo prominently displayed on the side. It just seems so much more prevalent and available in Japan.

Another attention to detail that I appreciate here is how passersby who find lost items, like keys or a dropped handkerchief, will pick it up and place it in a prominent place (high off the ground) so if the person who lost it returns can easily find it. If a "lost and found" office is available, a Good Samaritan will often return the item so the person who lost it can retrieve it. Again, this attitude goes back to politeness, and this polite behavior that is such an unshakable part of the Japanese psyche and culture is the oil that keeps the cultural and social machine in good running condition.

The "attention to details" that are so common in Japan makes daily life here seem more civilized. I certainly appreciate all the extras that people and companies do on a regular basis. It just makes for a better quality of life, knowing that someone, somewhere is thinking up yet other new ways to make the ordinary quite extraordinary.

[10] *Culture, People Top "List of Things Japanese"*

Saving the best until last, my tenth essay in this series is what makes Japan so special and why I consider it my second home: its culture and its people. Of course, there are nice people…and some not so nice people everywhere. Japan is no exception. Every culture has its positive attributes and not so great realities. For instance, a well-known trademark of Americans is friendliness with a sense of wanting to help one's fellow human being. Japanese people are widely considered to be a nation of very polite people, putting the "group" needs above one's individual needs, helping to keep society moving smoothly.

As expected, these examples are too simplistic, perhaps stereotypical, to be entirely accurate. There are many Americans who are not at all friendly and have little regard for the needs of others, and an equal number of Japanese who are impolite and self-centered. Lumping an entire group of people into one category is quite dangerous because differences—both positive and negative—do exist within any culture.

However, a number of people do make certain sweeping generalizations about a country and its people in order to make a point, tell a story, or to try to compare the minor differences rather than concentrating on the overwhelming amount of similarities. Making personal observations about a group of people is tricky, because it is filtered through one's own cultural attitudes, ideas, and experiences which have served to mold and define core characteristics of one's being and personality.

When I was a 17-year-old high school student, I remember an orientation session I attended as I prepared to go to Japan for the first time as an exchange student. The facilitator was trying to impress upon us the importance of seeing another culture not through our own eyes but to see it from an alternative perspective—through the eyes of the host culture's inhabitants.

He said that as we depart for Japan to experience its culture, food, customs, way of living, and lifestyle, we needed to take off our own cultural sunglasses. For example, if Americans wear yellow cultural sunglasses, and Japanese people wear blue cultural sunglasses, we will only see green if we fail to take off our own sunglasses before putting on the other culture's. This illustration impressed me so much that after nearly 35 years I still remember it as if it were yesterday. Too often, as a member of a specific cultural or ethnic group, we humans tend to focus on the cultural differences with the other groups without taking into account all the many similarities that various groups of people from different ethnic backgrounds share and have in common.

I have had the great fortune to live in North America, Central America, Europe and Asia. Although each place differed geographically, it was amazing to me how similar so many aspects of each culture's core characteristics were. Of course, many beliefs, rituals, customs and traditions were quite different, but the most basic of needs, desires, wants, and hopes were the same—the human aspect or the "humanity of culture." The intent behind the act is often the same in every culture—be it life's rituals surrounding the birth of a new baby, transition into adulthood, marriage, or funeral rites—all have commonalities in the purpose behind the ritual, custom, or tradition. So, when I say that I admire the Japanese as a people, it is of course on the most human of levels, but it is also with a sense of respect and appreciation for their cultural heritage that has served to make them who they are today.

Do I like everything about Japanese culture? No, just like I cannot accept every aspect of any other cultural group, including my own. No matter how hard one tries, it is difficult to not carry some sort of cultural baggage when crossing cultures. One's own culture is such an integral part of a person's essence and being that it is hard not to separate oneself from a lifetime of cultural ideas, attitudes and beliefs.

Recently a friend recounted to me a story about a relative who traveled to Hawaii. She said that the woman complained about how rude all the Japanese tourists were behaving, pushing and shoving, talking loudly, without regard to the others around them, etc. First, this surprised me that all the Japanese tourists were being rude, because many of the things she described seemed so out of character according to my experience with Japanese people. Second, it really surprised me because today Japanese are quite savvy and well-seasoned travelers, being courteous and aware of others around them. At least, this has always been my observation.

Then it occurred to me that perhaps the person mistook the tourists as being Japanese just because they were Asian. Erroneously, some Americans tend to think all Asians hail from the same place, and have the same cultural tendencies. It would be the same as putting Americans and Canadians in one category as being culturally one and the same. Perhaps since Japanese are more numerous in some parts of the country, and are frequent travelers to Hawaii, it was assumed the people were Japanese.

It used to drive me crazy when I first started living in Japan, and on trips home, acquaintances would ask me how I liked living in "China" and wondered if I could speak Chinese. Ignorance is the only possible explanation for such outrageous questions. I had never lived in China, and I certainly could not speak Chinese—because I lived in JAPAN.

In the 1950s when Americans first started to travel abroad, the moniker "ugly American" was used to describe obnoxious, loud, and culturally insensitive American travelers. Fast forward more than a half-century later, however, and we find that traveling internationally is not as uncommon as it once was. Americans have adapted over the years by blending in more readily to unfamiliar places, and have experienced a wide variety of travel, making the label incorrect.

The same is true of the Japanese. In the 1960s and 1970s when Japan was first becoming an industrialized and rich nation, tourists who had never ventured from the borders of this island nation were perceived as being rude and inconsiderate. Today, so many Japanese travel internationally that it is a routine part of their lives and not extraordinary like it was some forty or so years ago.

I suspect that the people my friend's relative encountered in Hawaii were probably not Japanese but most likely were from other Asian countries which in the last few years have found their economies booming, allowing ordinary citizens who previously never had an opportunity to travel abroad, to now visit international destinations. Just like the "ugly" Americans before, and their successors, the Japanese of the 60s and 70s, these newbie travelers will eventually acclimate themselves to international travel, and the appropriate etiquette associated with such travel will naturally become a part of who they are.

Which leads me to ponder what "rudeness" actually is? It is certainly in the eye of the beholder because perhaps culturally, what seemed like rudeness to the American woman in Hawaii was a natural part of the cultural being of the people she encountered. On their own linguistic and cultural turf, their behavior is probably quite acceptable and the norm. True, when in "Rome do as the Romans do," but I think we need to cut some slack to foreign visitors who venture to another country as tourists; perhaps they are not as seasoned in traveling as we are, and keep in mind that not so long ago we were the laughing stock of the world, being labeled as "ugly Americans" when in fact we were behaving according to our cultural norms and ideas of what we believed was culturally appropriate.

Part II:

Rites of Passage

[11] *Early Childhood Education*

The system of early childhood education in Japan is quite different than in other countries. There are basically two systems that are used in Japan with regard to early childhood education. From ages 0-6, children can be enrolled into a *hoikuen* (nursery) which are classified as "daycare centers." These are primarily geared toward the "welfare" of the child and are regulated by the Ministry of Welfare under the Child Welfare Law. The emphasis of *hoikuen* is to take care of the child physically and mentally. In contrast, the *youchien* (kindergarten) system, for children aged 3-6, is regulated by the Ministry of Education under the School Education Law of 1947. These schools are geared toward the education of children.

Supervised by their teacher, Japanese nursery school children play tug-of-war during recess outside

The *hoikuen* system is very convenient for working parents because the hours it can be utilized are quite flexible and much longer than the *youchien* system. A typical kindergarten allows children to stay up to six hours in a day, where as a *hoikuen* will allow children to come early and stay late each day, depending on the parents' schedule. The *youchien* fee for a child is fixed, and the price depends upon whether it is public or private. The *hoikuen* fee is based on the income of the parents, allowing lower-income families to have equal footing with more well-to-do families.

One aspect I personally find very interesting regarding the average nursery school in Japan is the practice of keeping a daily diary (*nikki*) that details the highlights of the child's day, from extraordinary to mundane events. The *nikki* features daily entries by both the parents and the teachers. The diary itself travels back and forth from home to school in the child's bag each day. Every afternoon during nap time, the teachers read what the parents wrote the night before, and then write about the child's day thus far for the parents to read later that evening. This diary system is an excellent way to keep parents and teachers abreast of the child's school and home life. A typical entry includes details about the child's daily routine: foods eaten, sleep habits, language development, playtime, and interactions with other children.

The following excerpts are two *nikki* entries written by the teacher for my friend's child, Satoshi:

> April 2006
>
> *This morning, Sakura-chan in Momo Class [1-2 year olds] was lying on the floor crying. As soon as Satoshi saw her, he went over, held her hand, and spoke gently to her. He really is becoming a big brother, isn't he? Later, out on the playground, he was pushing the trucks over to one corner, where he made a car park. Next to that, he was shoveling sand into a toy truck until it was piled high. He looked like a real workman!*

May 2006

Today we played outside all day. We went for a walk, and Satoshi was happy to see the 'koi-nobori' *[banners shaped like fish]. He showed them to me and kept saying 'fish.' After picking flowers, looking for insects, and enjoying lots of nature, we used big sheets of cardboard to slide down the grass hill. Satoshi really enjoyed it, sliding down again and again. When we were tidying up this afternoon, Satoshi was really helpful, working right up until we finished.*

Generally, the diary tends to focus only on the positive aspects of the child's life, with both parents and teachers including favorable content about the child. Interestingly, I was told by my friend, that—for example—if one's child is bitten by another child at school, the teacher will verbally inform the parent of the child bitten to explain and apologize about what happened. The parents of the child who did the biting may never be told.

Now, if a parent specifically inquires about their child, for example, "Little Koji has been biting his sister at home…does he do it here?" The Japanese teacher most likely will still try to give the situation a positive spin by replying, "Well, occasionally, but only when provoked." This is enough information, however, for the parent to know the situation and then decide how to deal with it at home. The idea behind this is that children will be children and it is most likely a phase the child is going through and it is best not to bring too much attention to the bad behavior.

My friend related to me that she has witnessed what she labeled "peer discipline" being used by teachers at her son's nursery school. Children are encouraged to intervene in other children's disputes as mini-mediators. Of course, the teacher would intervene if the dispute was really out of hand, but the teacher may watch from a distance and mention to another child, "Look over there…I wonder what they are going on about…?" The child often will volunteer to go over and check out what is happening, mediating the disagreement by encouraging the other two to stop their fussing.

In general, child rearing in Japan allows for more raucous behavior by small children to be tolerated than what other Western cultures may normally find acceptable. Discipline is rarely done, allowing small children a lot of freedom to act and behave as they wish. However, once they reach a certain age, societal pressure kicks in and children are expected to walk a straight and narrow line. By the time they are in junior high school, they have been transformed into obedient and respectful little individuals.

There is little wiggle room from around this age for any bad behavior; peers will quickly put wayward students in their place. In severe cases, students who do not fit in socially are bullied, and over the years, there have been a rash of junior high school children who commit suicide in Japan because of peer bullying—some physical and some mental.

This is a sad reality, indeed, considering how carefree and happy-go-lucky their lives most likely were when they were small children.

[12] *Coming of Age in Japan is a Big Celebration for Young Adults*

Every year, on the second Monday of January, Japanese young people from all over the archipelago attend a ceremony to mark their "coming of age" into adulthood *sei jin no hi*. On this day, young people (who turned 20-years-old over the past calendar year) dress up in their finest clothes—women in elaborate *kimono* and men mostly in dark business suits.

The men will wear these same suits to interview for jobs once they graduate from university, and women who choose to purchase a *kimono* and *obi* (sash) often wear it as one of the formal changes a bride makes on her wedding day. Many women, however, opt to rent a *kimono* for the day instead of incurring the huge expense to buy one for this ceremony. The *kimono* is worn so seldom nowadays that many women rent *kimonos* for this day, their graduation day, and for their wedding day. Taking into account the entire cost of the rental fees for the various occasions, although quite dear, is still cheaper than personally buying a high-grade pure silk *kimono* with an embroidered silk *obi*.

Municipalities all over Japan hold celebrations for the new adults with speeches by city dignitaries, receptions, and formal group photos. Young people return to their hometowns for the celebration, meeting up with old classmates to celebrate their adulthood together. In recent times, some changes have been made to attract more young people to attend these gatherings because interest in such activities has waned over the years. Traditionally, the speeches were sermon-like, pontificating about the importance of adulthood and the responsibility each new adult had to society.

Dressed in traditional *kimono*, 20-year-old women shop for an amulet at a shrine to celebrate "Coming of Age Day"

A few years ago the situation was so bad at one ceremony in a small town that a confrontation between the speaker and the attendees occurred, which is quite rare in Japan. The young adults were so bored that they began to chat loudly with each other and on their cell phones, causing the speaker to lash out with a tirade against the young adults, chastising them for their rude behavior. They booed him off the stage. At another ceremony, some boys engaged in tom-foolery by setting off firecrackers during the speech which caused a huge raucous. Currently, city offices around Japan are trying to update their activities to not only attract a higher number of young people to attend, but to make it more interesting for them by inviting more trendy speakers.

Young people today need to be entertained, I suppose, having been raised with technological gadgets and instantaneous gratification from overindulgent parents. Certainly the same is true in the West. The younger generation needs more bells and whistles to hold their interest for more than a few minutes; an old-fashioned dog and pony show just does not cut it in the new millennium.

Historically, the "Coming of Age Ceremony" has been observed in Japan since about the 7th century. Originally there was no particular age, but boys who reached the height of about 4.5 feet would embrace more mature, adult-like hairstyles and clothing; also they would receive adult names. This usually occurred anywhere between the ages of 10-16 with the ceremony being held at the discretion of the family. After the ceremony, the boy was considered to be a member of adult society, allowing him to participate in adult affairs, including religious ceremonies, and even marriage. Girls had a similar ceremony usually between the ages of 12-16.

Today, adulthood in Japan occurs at the age of 20. At this age, Japanese young adults can legally vote, drink alcohol, smoke tobacco, and gamble (Japanese young people are eligible to drive at the age of 18).

A popular tradition on Coming of Age Day is to visit a shrine or temple. Many years ago, I happened to be in Tokyo on this national holiday and visited Asakusa Shrine in central Tokyo. Groups of young men in suits and *kimono* clad women were scurrying up and down the narrow street leading to the shrine. Along this street, traditional shops line both sides. The young adults were buying mementos, like amulets and talismans, to commemorate their visit to this well-known shrine. This was a unique experience to see so many young people in their Sunday finest bantering about the shrine excited at being a full-fledged adult. I imagine the feeling is not too much unlike that of a young adult in the West turning 18 and graduating from high school, experiencing for the first time the responsibility of being "grown-up," at least in the eyes of society.

One difference, though—at least in the United States—is that the American young adult has to wait another three years in most states to be able to have a drink legally. In Japan, all rights and privileges of adulthood are give in one flail swoop at the age of 20.

[13] *Japanese Weddings are Unique and Memorable*

Attending a traditional Japanese *Shinto* wedding is quite a unique and memorable experience. I have attended a number of church weddings and Japanese-style receptions over the years while living here, but only once have I had the privilege of attending a traditional Shinto wedding ceremony.

Most Japanese consider themselves to be both *Shintoists* and Buddhists, usually opting for a *Shinto* wedding and a Buddhist funeral. Few cultures offer the opportunity to glide so easily between religions; but Japanese culture does, and aspects of both religious traditions are everywhere you look in Japan.

Many people maintain both a Buddhist altar and *Shinto* shrine in their homes. Many businesses will display a small *Shinto* shrine, as well as invite a *Shinto* priest to bless the construction of a new building. Families invite Buddhist priests to chant sutras during the *O-Bon* season (the August holiday where ancestral spirits are invited back to the home) and to perform ceremonies during the anniversaries of loved ones' deaths—combining and borrowing from both religious traditions.

A traditional *Shinto* wedding ceremony is beautiful in its solemnity and ritual. The bridal couple wears traditional costumes. The groom wears a *hakama* (a pleated pant-like garment) with a black *kimono* jacket. The family crest of the groom is usually emblazoned on each side of the upper front of the chest portion of the *kimono*.

The bride wears a pure white, delicately embroidered silk *kimono* (called a *shiromuku*) with long sleeves that reach past her knees. The

A Japanese bridal couple, dressed in traditional wedding *kimono*, during the *Shinto* wedding ceremony

long sleeves signify she is single; once married, she will only wear short-sleeved *kimonos* indicating that she is married.

The white color of the *kimono* dates back to the days of the *samurai* when a woman would show her submission to the family she was marrying into, conveying "I submit myself to you to be dyed any color to conform to your family's wishes and social standing."

In addition to her white *kimono* that drags around her feet as she walks, she wears elaborate white makeup and a traditional wig that most Westerners associate with that of what a *geisha* might wear. Over her wig, she wears a white silk covering. This headpiece is traditionally used to hide the bride's "horns of jealousy."

The ceremony is performed by a *Shinto* priest and is attended by two shrine maidens who assist in the ritualistic portion of the ceremony. Because *Shinto* is an animistic religion revering nature, dating to time immemorial, the ceremony reflects much symbolism connected to its nature-worship tradition.

The elaborate ritual surrounding the exchanging of nuptial cups of *sake*, though, is the most important part of a *Shinto* wedding. Blessings are bestowed upon rice wine (*sake*), where three cups are stacked neatly on a wooden stand near the *Shinto* priest and wedding couple. The bridegroom first takes the topmost cup and the shrine maiden delicately pours *sake* into the cup.

Carefully, the groom takes three small sips signifying *san-san-kudo* or the deepening of the relationship to form a stronger connection between the wedding couple. The groom then hands the cup to his bride and it is refilled and she repeats the ritual.

This is then reversed for the second cup, with the bride first partaking of the *sake* in three sips before handing it to the groom. Just as the first cup's ritual, the couple then each partakes of the *sake* from the third cup. Each guest in attendance also drinks a bit of the rice wine, further solidifying the new union which extends to the families.

Traditionally, *Shinto* weddings were held in actual shrines, but today most are held in hotels that have recreated exact replicas of shrines on the premises. I remember being awestruck when I arrived at the appointed room that looked to me like an ordinary banquet room from the outside; when the doors opened, however, a beautifully constructed wooden shrine, perfectly designed for wedding ceremonies, was revealed.

Unlike in some countries, this ceremony does not necessarily mean the couple is legally married. A secular registration at the city office (where the proper papers are submitted by the bride and groom) actually legalizes the union. The wedding itself, and the lavish reception that follows the ceremony, has no bearing whatsoever on the couple's legal status as husband and wife. It only becomes legal once the marriage notice (*konin todoke*) is submitted and registered, which is similar to the European tradition and custom of legalizing marriages.

A friend of mine once had a huge wedding party to satisfy her parents' desire that she marry before they died. It had all the makings of an authentic wedding, except she never registered it formally…and hence was not really married in the legal sense, just the social sense. Her parents were satisfied that the "appearance" of a marriage took place. They never knew that she and the man they thought she married never registered it with the city office. It also kept prying neighbors and relatives from gossiping about why she had not married even though she was past the normal marrying age.

Interestingly, a cottage industry has recently been created for foreigners to perform weddings in hotel and wedding hall chapels all over Japan. Just like the recreated shrines, hotels also offer the wedding couple the option of a "church" wedding—with an authentic looking country chapel and a foreign minister to perform the ceremony. The problem is that a goodly portion of the ministers who perform the weddings are English teachers with no ordination papers. Because the weddings are not legally binding and are mostly for show, there is nothing illegal about a person impersonating clergy or ministers in Japan. Besides, the majority of the couples who have "Christian" church weddings are not even Christian, but are Buddhist…or Shinto…well, probably both.

The reception that immediately follows the wedding ceremony (for both *Shinto* and Christian ceremonies) is often held in the same hotel where the wedding ceremony took place. Normally, the number of guests invited to the actual ceremony is strictly limited, but the reception's guest list is much larger, including close family members, extended family, friends, neighbors and work colleagues.

Being invited to a wedding reception is an honor. However, as a university professor, I cringe when the telltale thick envelope arrives in the mail. Not because I do not want to join in the joyous celebrations of former students, but because after decades of teaching here I receive a lot of invitations.

With each invitation, then, is the obligatory attendance fee (*oiwai*) that guests are expected to pay to attend the wedding reception. The closer the guest is to the couple, as well as the higher the social position of the guest, dictates the amount of money one should give to attend the reception. Wedding receptions in metropolitan areas, like Tokyo and Osaka, of course, generally command much higher fees.

Also, if the status of the family who is hosting the reception is fairly high, the reception can then become an opportunity for the guests to network between meal courses and speeches, making it an opportune time to make business contacts. So, a wedding in Tokyo can oblige a fee anywhere from $500-$1000 per person. This sounds outrageous, I know, but everything in Tokyo is more expensive, and wedding parties are no exception.

I live in rural Japan so the cost to attend a wedding party is at the bargain price of around $200-$500, again depending upon one's relationship to the couple and one's social status in the community. This "attendance fee" is in lieu of giving a gift to the couple and it goes toward paying for the lavish wedding reception and sumptuous meal served to the guests.

In appreciation, the couple then presents each guest with a "thank you gift" for attending the reception. Recently, it has become quite trendy for the couple to give each guest a catalogue from which to choose a gift of their own liking. A postcard is included that the person fills out with three possible selections in the order of what they want most. The catalogue company then processes the order and the item is delivered to the guest's door within a week or two.

In the past, the couple would select a gift to give the guests. The problem was that often it was something that may or may not be useful in a practical sense. This new system allows guests to choose things that they may really want or need. In the past, I have selected an electric wok from one reception, and a toaster oven from another. The "guest's gift" is usually valued at around $50.00.

As the wedding reception begins, the bridal couple is ushered into the banquet hall where all the guests are seated in assigned seats. Much care and discernment is taken in making the seating arrangements as not to offend those in attendance. The groom's company boss and bride's work supervisor are usually given the seats of honor at the front of the hall; next are the bridal couple's university professors who are seated in seats of honor.

The status and relationship of the guest to the couple are then taken into account as each person is seated from front to back—the front being the choice assignments, and the back being the least preferred. Unfortunately, the families of the couple are normally seated all the way in the back next to the kitchen door that is used by the hotel staff to serve the guests. By offering the choicest seats to the guests, the family demonstrates humility and a sense of humbleness.

Wedding receptions in Japan are notorious for their formality and stuffiness. The bride and groom, still dressed in the traditional costumes from the wedding ceremony are seated on a platform at the front of the hall with the *nakoudo*, the "go between" couple who traditionally were the ones that arranged the marriage. Today, "arranged marriages" in the traditional sense are much rarer than they were just 20 years ago, but the custom of having the matchmaker assist the couple during the party endures.

Next are the speeches. The honored guests, company bosses and university professors, make rather long speeches to the couple, giving advice to them about their future and wishing them a lifetime of wedded bliss. The speeches often have standard themes that encourage the couple to have children as quickly as possible. This always amuses me because the couple has yet to go on their honeymoon!

Once the toast is made, then the party may begin. In between courses, the couple is escorted out of the hall where the bride changes into several different wedding outfits. From the white *kimono*, she may change into a red *kimono*, leaving her wig and make-up on from the traditional ceremony. Next, she will often change into a formal evening gown with a hoop (the groom changes into a tux with tails). Finally, the wedding couple changes into western-style wedding attire at the end of the party.

While the couple is away changing, often times friends will entertain the guests with musical numbers, *karaoke*, or a professional band will play music. The guests meander about, beer bottle in hand, offering to refill other guests' beer glasses.

In Japan, it is customary not to fill your own glass with a beverage, but to wait for the person next to you to fill it for you. If your own glass is empty, and no one has noticed, all you have to do is to offer to fill the other person's glass. That person will then reciprocate by filling your glass. Also, it is polite to go to the platform and offer to refill the bridal couple's glasses of beer to show one's approval of the union.

The wedding reception lasts several hours, and when it is all said and done the total cost can be around $30,000-$50,000 for the wedding reception. Of course, the more guests that are invited, and the more changes the bride makes in and out of the rented gowns, increases the total cost.

Hence, when someone is invited to a wedding, the envelope never says "and guest." It would bankrupt a family of four to attend a wedding in Japan, not to mention upset the sitting arrangements. Only the person invited attends the wedding, leaving his/her spouse or significant other at home.

[14] *Divorce in Japan*

When I first came to Japan, divorce was still rather rare. Only occasionally did I meet someone who had divorced. Today, the numbers are catching up rather quickly with those in other Western countries.

It is still not as common here, and there tends to be a negative stigma still associated with divorce in Japan (especially towards women), but slowly society is making allowances for divorcées—primarily because of its prevalence and because people have no choice. More and more families are being touched by divorce, either directly or indirectly.

Divorce is quite easy in Japan. All that has to be done legally is for both people to have mutual consent; they must affix their personal seal (*hanko*) on an official form; and then have it registered at the city office. If both agree to it, then it is a done deal. There is no need to have a family court involved. It is accepted and settled upon filing.

This type of system is quite rare in most other countries and is probably one of the easiest in the world. I read where about 90% of couples in Japan divorce in this manner. The idea of "joint custody" is a totally foreign concept in Japan. Recently I assigned students in my culture class an article to read about an American family that showed just how complicated a joint custody arrangement can be. The parents were jostling and arguing about whose turn it was to have the child that week. The boy in the article seemed bewildered and sedately resigned to the process as his parents divided his time between them.

This system is so common in the US that kids do not think anything about being ferried from parent to parent each week, on weekends, separate but equal vacation time, etc. It is but one aspect of American family life that has become ordinary to a certain extent. In Japan, there is no system of "joint custody" and this could be due to cultural reasons. Legally, only one parent after the divorce has sole custody and this largely has to do with the fact that the parents no longer are legally bound to one another, so they are viewed by society as being completely separate.

The parent who does not have custody is expected to participate in the financial cost of raising the child by sharing the expenses associated with the child. This is usually the father. An overwhelming majority of custody cases in Japan are awarded to the mother.

The parent who does not have custody is allowed visitation, but it is not expressly stipulated in the divorce settlement. It is considered a natural right of a parent to be able to see his/her child, call by telephone, or exchange letters. There is no "legal provision" for these types of contacts but is allowed as a matter of precedent and practice.

It is my observation, though, that often the parent who does not have legal custody generally does not see his/her children regularly, if ever. Once the marriage is severed legally, it seems that all association is then cut off, except for financial remuneration as a sort of "support" payment. This, too, is difficult at times for the custodial parent to force the other parent to contribute financially if the other parent refuses.

Interestingly, with more and more Japanese marrying foreigners, it is only logical that a certain percentage of these marriages end in divorce. This is causing the courts to rethink some of the customs associated with divorce because Westerners, especially North Americans, want and demand some sort of "joint custody" arrangement. At times, it does leave judges scratching their heads trying to figure out how to solve amicably these types of disputes.

A recent Japanese trend that is somewhat surprising is the high percentage of divorces between couples who are in their "golden years;"

after the children are raised and on their own, a number of couples (after decades of marriage) decide to call it quits. Perhaps the children were the bond that held the couple together, and when they finished raising the children, they were at a loss at how to interact with the other, one on one.

Also, traditionally, with the husband working outside the home—often married to his career, spending most days, evenings and weekends with work colleagues—the wife feels her personal space is invaded when he does retire and sometimes decides not to spend the rest of her life serving him. So, she seeks a divorce.

I saw a talk show where a woman in her 60s was talking about her divorce. She said that when her children were at home, then in college, she had a purpose. But, when her children married and her husband retired from his job, she decided that she preferred to be alone rather than to have to put up with him every day. When he worked, she felt she had some freedom to do as she pleased, but after he was home day in and day out, she could not stand to be around him.

For every older couple that divorces, there are probably several couples that have worked out a sort of divorce without legally going to the trouble to dissolve the marriage. These couples often live in the same home but live separately. The wife may live in the downstairs and the husband upstairs, never exchanging greetings, and going about their lives as if they were divorced. This system allows them to save face by not going through the actual public humiliation of a divorce—the neighbors are none the wiser, most likely, thinking that everything is normal, when in fact the husband and wife are (for all practical reasons) "divorced."

There is also a stigma associated with the children of divorced parents in Japan. Often parents wanting to divorce will wait until all of their children are married before filing. No upstanding family wants their child to marry someone from a divorced family, as if it were something contagious. So, they live in misery, putting on a happy façade until the children marry, then they divorce.

A Japanese friend was being pressured to get married by his mother—not because she necessarily wanted to have grandchildren but because she was anxious to divorce his father. As soon as he married, it was only a matter of months before his parents divorced.

In my opinion, Japanese women in Japan certainly get the short end of the stick in divorces. There are a number of derogatory terms used toward women, such as *demodori* which refers to a woman who goes back to her parents' home after the divorce. Another term, *kizumono*, means "damaged goods" like those that are on a discount table because they likely cannot be sold again—"seconds," in other words. A more modern term used for both men and women is *batsu ichi* meaning "one failure," like the English term "one strike." These terms are quite harsh, so it is understandable why people here are hesitant to divorce, even those who desperately need to, because of the stigma associated with them afterwards by society.

In America, the majority of divorced people eventually remarry, but in Japan, this is not the case. Younger people are more apt to remarry, but the majority of middle-aged to older Japanese who divorce often do not remarry. Perhaps they do not want to chance it again.

[15] *Funeral Rituals Differ in Protocol and Etiquette*

A woman attends to the family grave at a Japanese cemetery

A friend wrote to me regarding the proper way to offer one's condolences to a Japanese person who has suffered the loss of a loved one. This person's friend had lived in the US and has since returned to Japan. A series of tragedies had befallen her Japanese friend, including the death of a beloved pet. The person wanted to know how to pay respect to her Japanese friend in a way that is culturally sensitive with regards to Japanese protocol and etiquette.

Every culture has strict and elaborate social rules regarding funeral ceremonies, and Japan, like other countries, is no different in this respect. Japan, however, tends to be less flexible when it comes to making gaffes when observing certain funeral-related rituals.

For instance, in the United States, funeral customs have undergone tremendous cultural changes from the way people dress to attend a funeral, to what types of offerings are made in the form of flowers, plants, and keepsake gifts (things given to the family in memory of the deceased person).

Even the styles of services have metamorphosed greatly with "celebrations of the person's life" often taking place instead of the morose funerals of yesteryear. All in all, modern American funeral rituals have become much less formal in recent years and offer people attending funerals a lot more leeway in the etiquette department.

Not so in Japan. Japanese funerals are still very formal with a prescribed protocol that is strictly followed. For instance, Japanese people dress very formally to attend the wake, funeral, or cremation ceremony. Each attendee dresses from head to toe in black. Men even don a black tie to wear with their tuxedo-like suits. Anyone who sees a man wearing a black tie knows he is on his way to, or has just been to, a funeral.

In contrast, a man wearing a black suit with a white tie is either on his way to, or is returning from, a wedding. The tuxedo-like suit doubles for both occasions; the color of the tie is what makes the difference.

Women usually opt to wear very plain (but formal) black dresses. These dresses are unique in that usually they are not at all fashionable, but are often boxy and drab in appearance. It would be disrespectful to stand out at such an event due to stylish apparel. Matching black handbags and shoes are also worn. Japanese women will also wear black dresses to weddings, but these are usually stylish with colorful accessories. A woman attending a funeral wears no added color with the exception of maybe pearls, which are sometimes gray in color.

Even the meal that is served to the attendees at a wake is comprised of foods that are muted in color. *Sushi* and *sashimi* (raw fish) are rarely served at funeral-related dinners because of their bright and happy colors. Only once have I attended a funeral where *sashimi* was served. It was for a well-known politician who was once the Defense Minister and Agriculture Minister; with so many important people in attendance, social-protocol required that the meal be of the highest quality, which meant *sashimi* should be served. The way the caterers maneuvered around this cultural conundrum was to wrap the plate of *sashimi* lightly with a gray colored paper to hide the bright colors.

It is appropriate to offer flowers to people who have suffered a loss, but the flowers should be subdued in color and have no scent to them at all. Bright, garish colors are considered inappropriate at funerals with white chrysanthemums being the flower of choice. Scented flowers in bright colors are reserved for only happy, joyous occasions in Japan.

When I first lived in Japan as a 17-year-old high school student, I shocked my host mother with a gift of funeral flowers. I had no idea there was a difference—after all, to me, flowers were flowers.

On my way home from the grocery one day, I passed a sweet old lady who was selling beautiful bunches of mums. I thought it would be nice to surprise my host mother with a bouquet of flowers. Well, she was definitely surprised all right. I will never forget her facial expression when I waltzed into the house with my offering of funeral flowers. She was horrified. I had no idea what I had done wrong, but I knew something was amiss because of her strangely nervous reaction to my gift.

Immediately, she went into the kitchen, hurriedly snipped the stems, then took them directly to the *tatami* (straw mat) room and placed them inside the very ornate and imposing Buddhist altar. She lit some incense, gonged a bell, and prayed fervently. Now I was really worried. What had I done?

When my host brother arrived home that evening, he quickly asked me why I had brought his mother "those" flowers earlier in the day. Still not knowing, I sheepishly queried "just to be nice?" It was then that he realized that I had not the foggiest idea that I had committed a huge faux pas regarding this rather obscure custom. How was I supposed to know that certain flowers are only reserved for the dead?

In answering the original question from my friend, however, I think any Japanese person receiving a condolence card or a bouquet of flowers from a foreign friend would be touched. The person would be even more impressed if the flowers were in accordance with Japanese funeral customs, and the card included a handwritten message of sympathy.

Fortunately for us, we foreigners are given a lot of leeway in the etiquette department when it comes to observing certain customs that are Japanese-based. Japanese people sometimes have a difficult time deciphering all of the intricacies of their own customs and traditions. For me, though, I have been here long enough to know better. I am expected to be aware of, and know what is proper and correct...and what is not. Consequently, my offering of funeral flowers to my host mother was only the first of many cultural gaffes that I have since committed during my tenure in Japan.

In Japan, it is customary and socially correct to make an offering of money to the deceased person's family when attending a funeral. This money is called *koden*, with the amount given dependent upon how close you were to the person, your social position in the community, and/or your own financial ability. The usual amount of money offered is around $30-$50. It is extremely important that the money given is put in a special envelope that has black and white cords elaborately tied around it. Also, the bills should be old and well-worn—not new.

Offering a new bill as a funeral offering could give the appearance that the death was expected and you had time in advance to prepare "new" bills for the occasion. The opposite is true when offering money to a wedding couple; only new, yet to be circulated bills, should be given. This shows that you made a special effort to visit the bank in order to prepare crisp new bills which shows you approve of the wedding. Used bills for a wedding could convey that you are not that pleased about the union.

The subtlety involved in these types of cultural practices make it very hard for an outsider not to offend people on some level. These cultural-cues are based on a long tradition, practiced amongst a very homogenous group of people. Japanese people intuitively know such implied hints, and can read a situation instantly, relying on their own cultural background and knowledge "to do the right thing." Outsiders like me, on the other hand, must fumble around and learn by trial and error.

In the case of a place like America, with its patchwork quilt of ethnic groups, could never have such indirect customs due to the wide variety of cultural backgrounds that have fused together to make the United States the country it is today. It is doubtful that an American bridal couple would give it any thought at all if someone gave them a $100 bill that had been in circulation; the hidden meaning, so apparent in Japan, would have to be more direct for Americans to get it (e.g. putting no money in the envelope—now that would get the couple's attention).

The cost of a funeral in Japan, like in most countries, can be exorbitantly expensive. The monetary offering paid by each attendee helps to defray the cost incurred upon the family. In return, in order to cancel out any obligation to the person giving the monetary gift, the family then prepares a small gift for the attendees as a token of their profound appreciation for the generosity extended to them.

These gifts are usually valued at $15-$20, and are wrapped in white, gray or black paper; usually included in the gift-bag is a note of appreciation from the family. The attendees are handed these gifts as they leave the funeral. In the past, I have received telephone cards, coupons to exchange for rice, handkerchiefs, noodles, and hand towels in such instances. Japanese social etiquette requires that a gift of money be reciprocated, in some way, hence the reason why the family is obliged to offer guests a token gift at the funeral or soon after.

In addition, it is important for the attendees to write on the offering envelope in very light, even gray ink. Again, to use a rich, dark ink would suggest that the death was expected and the person writing had ample time to prepare the ink from an ink-stone. In the old days, it took much time and effort to prepare the *sumi* (ink) to write letters. Using gray ink conveys that the death was such a shock that the person had no time to concoct properly the ink, hurriedly mixing it, resulting in a dull, grayish colored ink. A woman at the university where I teach is a master calligrapher and she is always ready and willing to help me with these calligraphy-related duties. When she writes on a funeral envelope, it is ever so light and her writing is so beautiful—a work of art. My Japanese writing, in contrast, looks like it was done by a three-year-old.

Nowadays, stores offer a huge assortment of items to make these necessary tasks easier. One can purchase a pen that automatically writes in a grayish ink. All supermarkets and convenience stores have a section that sells the various types of envelopes needed for these culture-specific obligations. Just as there is an assortment of envelopes for funerals, there are those for weddings and other happier occasions that come in red, white and gold.

The more elaborate envelopes signify the amount of money placed inside them. It would be strange to use a highly decorated envelope with only a small amount of money placed inside it. So, there are all kinds of envelopes to choose from—the very plain to the ostentatious—depending upon the size of your offering.

Funeral customs in Japan are steeped in tradition that often go back to ancient times. Of course, the burial custom in Japan is to cremate the deceased and then place the ashes in a family altar at a gravesite (and not bury the person in the ground, like in many countries). This custom has its origins in Buddhism, but is also done out of practicality. The scarcity of available land and the exorbitant cost of land, makes it impractical to bury people in individual plots.

Part III:

Japanese Festivals and Celebrations

[16] *New Year's in Japan*

New Year's Day in Japan most resembles Christmas Day in the United States in that it is a family holiday where relatives travel from near and far to celebrate the holiday together. Before New Year's Eve, Japanese family members begin to arrive at their ancestral home to prepare for the New Year, just like American families do before Christmas.

Oshougatsu, or New Year's, is by far the most important and most celebrated of any of Japan's annual events. Most Japanese workers are given from December 30-January 3 off from their jobs in order to be with their families during this holiday. Before leaving work at the end of December, though, offices and schools all over Japan do a thorough and complete cleaning. This *osoji* is a deep cleaning that requires pulling out desks and bookshelves from the walls to clean every nook and cranny, throwing out unused items, and making sure all is arranged back nicely for the New Year. Many families do a similar cleaning of homes at the end of the year to make everything fresh and clean to bring in the New Year.

One custom that I have adopted here in Japan during the New Year celebration is the tradition of *hatsu-moude* or the first shrine or temple visit of the New Year. At midnight, on New Year's Eve, I bundle up in warm clothes and traipse out into the bitter cold to the local *Shinto* shrine with friends to pay my respects.

The atmosphere at the shrine is always jovial and happy; people are excitedly buying lucky arrows, talismans, and amulets to ensure they have good luck and good health throughout the next year. As the hoards of people make their way to the front of the shrine, everyone takes a turn to clap their hands and offer a coin offering to the *kami* or gods. Not all people visit a shrine at midnight on New Year's Eve, thank goodness, as there would be no space to move. Officially, one can visit a temple or shrine until around January 7th in order to get the full effect of good fortune throughout the next year.

Many years ago, I spent the New Year's holiday in Tokyo with a friend's family. On New Year's Day we took a bus, then a couple of trains, to get to the most famous of all shrines in Japan—Meiji Shrine. I have never in my life seen more people crammed into a finite space. The momentum of the crowd carried us to the front as we feebly tried to toss our coins against the surge of people pushing us by. It was actually scary because if anyone had fallen, surely the person would have been trampled to death.

I prefer visiting the temple near my home. I nearly always run into a number of people I know—colleagues and neighbors—which allows us to exchange verbal New Year's greetings to one another. *Akemashite omedetou gozaimasu* is the common Japanese phrase used to wish someone a "Happy New Year." Huge bells at Buddhist temples are gonged 108 times, starting at midnight, to chase away the evils or worldly desires of the past year. From north to south, famous temples all over Japan are featured on public television, showing the priest of the temple solemnly ringing the bell.

Why the number "108"? There are many legends related to why this number is significant, but a common belief is that it represents 12 + 24 + 72. Of course 12 is representative of each month of the year; the number 24 signifies the points of an ancient East Asian lunar-solar calendar; and 72 is an ancient Chinese custom that divided the year into three sections of 24. No one really knows definitively why this is done, only that it is tradition and it has always been done in this way.

Japanese children—from toddlers to university students—anxiously anticipate New Year's Day because they are given *o-toshidama*, a small envelope with money, by adult relatives and friends. This custom is akin to Christian kids receiving presents on Christmas Day.

It is hard to know how much is appropriate, but I generally give 100 yen for each year of the child's age. This is a custom I started with my nephew, giving him $1 for each year of his age on his birthday. When he turned eight, he was quite excited when 8 one-dollar bills tumbled out of his birthday card.

Similarly, my cost-effective system seems to work well here. Actually, 100 yen is a not actually a dollar, but is the closest denomination to an American buck. So, taking into consideration yearly inflation, I figure this gradual yearly increase of cold, hard cash is probably about as fair as any; when the kids turn 20-years-old, they can expect around $20.

Homes all around my neighborhood display *shimenawa* (a sacred rope of straw with small strips of white paper dangling down) on the front doors. This is to distinguish the home as being one that is a temporary domicile for the *toshigami* or New Year deities that visit the home during this season; it is also used to discourage any malevolent spirits from entering the home.

A typical New Year's Day meal (*osechi ryouri*) is served in stackable lacquered boxes filled with a variety of Japanese delicacies. These specialty foods are highly preserved, hence prepared well in advance of the day, eliminating the need to spend endless hours in the kitchen cooking during the first few days of the New Year.

Popular and traditional foods include stewed black soybeans, salted herring roe, dried sardines cooked in soy sauce, cooked burdock marinated in vinegar, broiled fish paste, sweet omelet squares, broiled shrimp, sea bream, radish (*daikon*) salad, and all daintily garnished with brightly colored vegetables and fruits.

Traditional Japanese New Year's foods in stackable lacquered boxes

Many families purchase ready-made *osechi ryouri* (as do I) at their local supermarket, or order the boxed meal in advance from a favorite restaurant, which cuts the preparation time down even more. These are delicately arranged in faux lacquer boxes.

Every year I bring in the New Year with my nearest and dearest in typical Japanese fashion. I do, however, plan to have some traditional American New Year dishes mixed in with the traditional Japanese ones. Salted herring, broiled fish paste, and black soy beans will not satiate this Hoosier's love of honeyed ham, macaroni and cheese, and corn beef and cabbage!

[17] *Valentine's Day in Japan a One-Sided Affair*

Valentine's Day is an occasion when sweethearts all over the world give their special someone a card, flowers, chocolates or a special gift. Not so in Japan. The Japanese custom of Valentine's Day is celebrated much differently than in other cultures. Traditionally, at least in the United States, it is the man who gives chocolates and presents to the woman. In Japan, it is exclusively the woman who gives chocolates to the man. Of course, many women around the world on this day give tokens of their affection to men and vice versa, but in Japan it is only women who give these things to men.

There are basically two attitudes regarding the giving of chocolate by women to men in Japan: *giri choco* ("obligatory" chocolate) and *honmei choco* ("from the heart" chocolate). Many women who work in offices feel "obligated" to give all the men they work with—from their boss to ordinary coworkers—chocolate on Valentine's Day. This obligation to give chocolates to men has made some Japanese women very resentful of this custom. Men have come to expect chocolate on Valentine's Day from OLs (the Japanese term for "office ladies"). Often women feel they have to give *giri choco* to all of the men and not just the ones they genuinely like.

Pressure to conform to the whims of the group can be very strong in Japanese society; a woman who does not follow through with this obligation may be looked down upon by her coworkers, especially the women, because she did not adhere to the accepted social protocol of this adopted holiday. A dear Japanese friend of mine who works in a well-known company absolutely detests this custom, but nevertheless presents a small wrapped box of chocolates each year to all the men in her office with a smile. The risk of being shunned is too great for her, so she succumbs to the social pressure, and dutifully performs this obligation unwillingly.

A new trend, though, that has been willingly adopted by a number of Japanese women, especially high school and university students, is *tomo choco* or "friendship chocolate." Women are now exchanging chocolate with their closest female friends as a sign of friendship. This chocolate is not only appreciated, but often immediately reciprocated, making the giver and receiver happy and content.

In recent years, however, the *giri choco* tradition has lost some steam due to the languishing Japanese economy that has been in the doldrums for many years now. Gradually, some women have stopped giving chocolates due to the sheer cost of performing this yearly ritual. Generally, a box of chocolates designated as *giri choco* can be purchased for around $2-$4 (these usually have 4-6 pieces). If a woman has ten male coworkers, this quickly adds up to a pretty pricey formality.

I am quite sure, though, that before a personal decision is made, the women in any given office will casually broach the subject before Valentine's Day with one another in order to gauge where everyone else stands on the issue. If the majority is in favor of not passing out chocolates, the group opinion would then prevail, and the men would be chocolate-less on the big day.

From mid-January, department stores, convenient stores, and supermarkets begin to display chocolates prominently to cash in on this peculiar tradition. The real winners, besides the men who can collect a dozen or more boxes of chocolate on this day, are the chocolatiers and confectioners in Japan who really promote this holiday in a big way.

Usually included next to the *giri choco* display is a section with all the makings and ingredients necessary to make homemade chocolate candy and cakes. This area is largely for the *honmei* ("from the heart") chocolate buyers who want to give a more sincere, handmade chocolate-based gift to their special someone. A female office worker normally would not go to all the trouble to make homemade chocolates for male coworkers, but she would put forth the extra effort for a beau or sweetheart. Either way, Valentine's Day is big business in Japan, but the hoggish chocolate industry cleverly thought of yet another way to further exploit the concept of *giri choco*.

Exactly one month after Valentine's Day, on March 14th, another holiday is celebrated that is uniquely Japanese—"White Day." This holiday was created in the early 1980s to give the men who received chocolate on Valentine's Day an opportunity to reciprocate the deed by giving the women who presented them with "dark" chocolate with "white" chocolate. Of course, this holiday was most likely created by the chocolate industry. So, as soon as February 14th is over, the same displays are converted into cutesy, feminine spectacles featuring white chocolate gifts for women.

I once took a poll in my class and asked how many of my university women students gave chocolate to men on Valentine's Day; a goodly number of women raised their hands. I then asked the men students in my class how many of them received chocolate on February 14th—again, the majority of them raised their hands. I finished by asking the men how many of them reciprocated the Valentine's chocolate they received with White Day chocolates. Not one hand went into the air.

This speaks volumes about the roles of men and women in Japanese society—women are expected to offer chocolates in February to their coworkers and feel obligated to do so, but men rarely feel guilty for accepting chocolates without returning the favor in March. The social expectation is completely different for men and women.

Still, for me, a big box of chocolates from my special someone, given from the heart, is much more appreciated than a bunch of small boxes of chocolate given out of duress. After all, just because a Japanese man receives numerous *giri choco* does not mean he has any real admirers. For all he knows, the female office worker bought the chocolate after Valentine's Day the year before at half-price, and presented it to him the next year…with a smile.

[18] *Girls' Day and Boys' Day Celebrations*

Hina Matsuri or "Girl's Day" is a doll festival held every year on March 3rd in Japan. This celebration recognizes everything girlish, allowing little girls to be little girls. A common practice is for girls to dress up in traditional kimono to entertain their friends with special treats—*hishimochi* (diamond shaped rice cakes). The idea is to sit and admire the meticulously displayed doll collection arranged on a multi-tiered platform. These dolls are never played with in the bathtub or the sandbox. They are much too delicate to be touched routinely.

A complete collection usually has around 15 dolls. The two main dolls, representing the emperor and empress, are always placed on the top tier dressed in traditional court costumes, flanked on both sides by miniature lanterns, with beautiful gold screens behind them. Arranged on the lower levels is their retinue: attendants, handmaidens, and court musicians. Interspersed on each of the lower levels are accouterments associated with the emperor and empress—chests, tables with food, musical instruments, and even an ox-drawn carriage.

Frequently a little girl's doll set is given to her by her mother, who had hers given to her by her mother. It is often a generational heirloom, with each new owner adding to the collection. It is displayed much like a Christmas tree is in that it is only to be admired, not touched, and stays set up for around two weeks before it is taken down It is then carefully packed away until the next year when the process is repeated.

During this season, many department stores have doll sets for sale. I was shocked at how expensive it is to purchase a complete set. The prices ranged from two-thousand to several-thousand dollars. This is why many families combine older pieces that have sentimental value with newer pieces as little girls are born into the family.

Neighbors once invited me to their home to partake in this celebration. The little girl, around 5-years-old, was so proud to show me her collection. She pointed out each piece explaining who and what it was. We all then sat and had refreshments while gazing at this most spectacular display of craftsmanship and tradition.

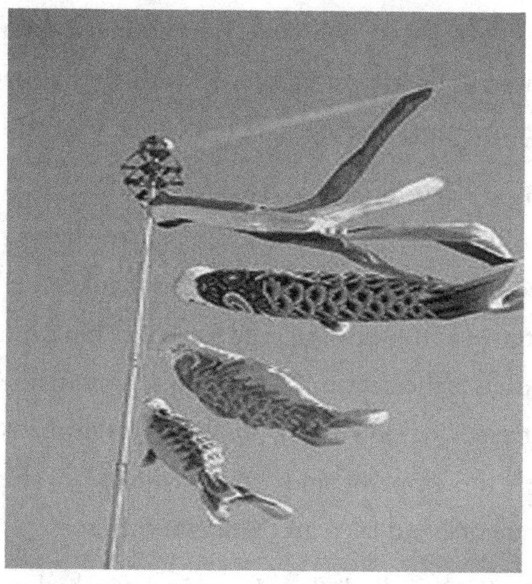

Koinobori banners being displayed for "Children's Day[2]

Not to be left out, boys also celebrate their own day in Japan on May 5th, *kodomonohi* (also called "Children's Day"). To mark this day, families who have boys fly huge carp-shaped streamers on poles outside their homes. These banners are called *koinobori* in Japanese and represent manly virtues, because the carp is such a hardy and gallant fish.

The tradition is actually Chinese in origin and is related to a Chinese myth about a carp that swam upstream and magically became a dragon. Japan had long considered the carp to be special in its own lore, so this just added to its appeal.

The size and number of carp banners flying outside a Japanese home represents the age and number of boys living in the household. Of course, the longest streamer (up to 15 feet in length) symbolizes the oldest son; the next biggest size is the second son, and so on. Even people who live in apartments will display shorter versions in graduated order according to how many sons the family has.

I have also heard the story that the carp represent the father, mother and son—the father carp being the biggest, the next being the mother, and the small one, the son. A friend told me that he remembers singing a song in kindergarten about the three carp and how they represent the family.

In recent years, some modern Japanese families have adapted the custom to include all of their children by displaying a flag for each child—not only for sons but also for daughters. Purists, of course, stick to the segregation of the sexes, celebrating Girls' Day with dolls, and Boys' Day with flying carps.

Both events are spectacular in different ways. The dolls are exquisite examples of master craftsmanship and the carp streamers look so majestic blowing in the wind high above the ground. Westerners are attracted to both types of objects because of their "Japaneseness."

Many years ago, an American friend living here thought that the banners would make a unique and interesting shower curtain. The problem was the carp banners were cut and sewn in such a way that made it difficult to convert them into a shower curtain easily.

She decided to write the company that makes the carp and asked to buy a set that had not been cut and sewn. The company was so impressed with her idea that they gladly sent her the unsown, uncut cloth of the carps free of charge. She now has quite the conversation piece after guests use her beautifully accented bathroom.

[19] *Goodbye Parties Tearful but Signal New Beginnings*

After over twenty-five years of living and being associated with Japan, I still occasionally have a strong dose of culture shock that leaves me scratching my head. This occurred at one of our annual *sobetsukai* (farewell party) for staff and faculty who left their positions at the end of March.

In Japan, April 1st marks the beginning of the fiscal year, so it is a time of new beginnings. The Japanese school year is on an April-July schedule for the first term (and October-February for the second term). Companies also follow this system, which means new employees begin working on April 1st, and staff that either transfer, change positions, or retire leave at the end of March.

Every year a number of faculty members from my university retire or accept positions at new institutions, so they leave to pursue their new careers. Also, several administrative staff people are transferred to different offices under the umbrella of the university including the attached junior and senior high schools.

This year's farewell party was especially teary-eyed and emotional for several of the administrative staff when they went on stage to give their short farewell speech. Several could not finish, apologizing profusely as they scurried away from the microphone. What made it so culturally interesting for me is that these people really are not leaving, but are only moving offices. Our university is compact and small, unlike mega-university campuses elsewhere, so the probability of seeing these people frequently is a statistical certainty.

So, why was everyone boo-hooing as if they were being exiled to a remote part of the country with no opportunity to see their colleagues ever again? After all, they are basically just changing offices, sometimes only a matter of feet away from where they were before. I have been pondering this cultural conundrum and have come to the conclusion that they are not necessarily mourning leaving the actual position as much as they are sad to be losing a familiar "group identity" and "history" that was associated with their prior position.

Of course, they will gradually identify with their new group of peers and colleagues, and after working in the new position for a while will eventually develop a history with these people as well. However, when the "history" associated with working, sharing, and bonding with those in the prior position ends, a new history has to be made with new people, new surroundings, with new duties and responsibilities. This can be quite daunting, especially if the person was quite happy in the position and not at all thrilled about being moved.

Partly, it also may be related to the fact that often transfers are told to the people a day or so before the farewell party, so there is an element of shock connected with the forced transfer. Change is hard for anyone, but it is especially so in a system where people are transferred at the behest of the institution or company and not because they necessarily want to move or change positions.

When I first came to Japan, this system of forced-transfer was hard for me to understand. At the junior high school where I taught, there was a certain tension in the air in mid-March as teachers fretted over whether they would be allowed to stay another year, or be transferred to another school—sometimes to the opposite end of the prefecture which meant they would have to relocate.

I was also assigned to a local board of education office where the same system was used. No one knew for sure if they would be staying or leaving. Once they were informed, it was often a matter of days before they had to get their desks packed up, find new places to live, and to participate in the obligatory "farewell party."

In these instances, it is understandable why people may be sad to leave because they most likely will not see their old colleagues regularly and everything that was familiar to them will be different with new surroundings, workmates and locations.

This system of "transfer" is called *tenkin* in Japanese and is practiced by nearly all businesses, educational institutions, and organizations that have multiple departments or locations within the same structure. The idea is to give employees a chance to experience a variety of duties within a company or institution, exposing them to as many facets of the organization as possible.

Sometimes the transfers seem illogical. A friend of mine who has a degree in library science was moved from his university library position to a clerk position in the testing center. His departure left a huge, gaping hole in the library as he was the most skilled person to handle the new technology associated with modern libraries. He resigned because he was so distraught at being moved from a position he loved and was skilled at doing, to one he hated (and had no experience at doing).

In the United States, of course, when people are promoted it may mean a change in environment, but usually an employee chooses whether to apply for another position within a company, hence is in control of where s/he works to a certain degree.

In Japan, school teachers rarely have a choice and feel obligated to transfer when the edict to do so comes from above. In the case of

US school teachers, the majority work their entire careers in the same school without changing. The custom in Japan, especially with younger teachers, is to move them every few years.

A related system is *tanshin funin* which literally means "to proceed to a new post alone." Companies will often relocate workers (usually men) to other locations, domestically or internationally, for a period of a couple of years or longer. Some of the reasons why families do not relocate with the "father" have to do with the cost that would be incurred by the company to do so; the hassle of having the children change schools which could be very disruptive with regard to their educational goals; the possibility of extended family members living with the nuclear family; and/or the hesitance to sell what is considered an ancestral home.

But, back to the original topic at hand, "farewell parties" are certainly not unique to Japan. When I worked for the state government as a summer intern during college, we often had farewell parties for people retiring or leaving. One big difference, however, was how happy the people retiring were compared to their Japanese counterparts. The majority of Americans relish the idea of retiring, even opting for early retirement if possible.

In Japan, retirees have a much different attitude toward this concept and often choose to continue working well into their 70s. A number of professors at my university have officially retired, but continue to teach and work. Again, they are hesitant to give up their "history" or "group identity" to embark upon something new and unfamiliar.

As I fast-forward 20 years to my retirement party, I doubt very much if I will be shedding any tears at leaving, unless of course they are tears of joy at finally being able to retire. No matter how much I acculturate to Japan, deep-down I am still very American because the thought of retiring is so exquisitely tantalizing.

[20] *Cherry Blossom Season in Japan a Sight to Behold*

My favorite activity in Japan, every year, is *hanami* (cherry blossom viewing). The area where I live always enjoys cherry blossom season around Golden Week, a series of national holidays that occur at the end of April and the beginning of May. Commencing in March, from south to north, all across Japan, cherry trees blossom and an annual ritual takes place—the viewing of the blossoms while eating and drinking from beneath their branches.

If there were a list of customs and rituals that—when combined—formed the "soul" of Japan, cherry blossom viewing parties certainly would rank high on the list. Colleagues from universities and schools, coworkers from companies, members of clubs, and just about any other combination of people, gather to enjoy the delicate pink blossoms swaying over their heads.

Enjoying the cherry blossoms at Hirosaki Castle during the annual festival

In companies, the new recruits are sent out early in the morning on the appointed day to scout out the best spots for viewing. Large plastic sheets are spread out and anchored down in preparation for the big event. The young staff members then guard the spot the entire day until nightfall when their coworkers arrive with the food and copious amounts of alcohol.

If the food is not carried in by the attendees, it is often catered by one of the many restaurants or bars that do a booming business during this season. Besides viewing the blossoms, the main attraction is to drink beer while eating traditional foods. As the night progresses, inevitably someone will stand up to do an impromptu dance or to sing a song. In fact, some groups even tote portable karaoke machines so they can sing to their hearts' content.

Usually after several hours, the party moves on to a *niji kai* or second party held at a pre-designated bar or pub, allowing everyone to continue their partying until the wee hours of the morning. Often, a viewing party will take place on a work night, so the blossom viewers are often a little worse for wear when they drag into their offices the next morning.

My first blossom viewing party was attended by teachers and staff at the board of education office where I worked. The organizers had thought of every detail. In anticipation of the likely hangovers, they gave everyone an energy drink which is widely used here as a cure-all for the morning after. Amazingly, not one person called in sick and no one complained about having a headache. There must be something to those energy drinks.

University students can sometimes go overboard with the drinking aspect because the cherry blossom season occurs shortly after classes begin in April. Too often, excessive drinking leads to alcohol poisoning so ambulances standby ready to assist in any over-indulgence that may occur or to assist in other types of medical emergencies. Every year, city offices place posters in and around university campuses to warn of the dangers of overdrinking. A game which educators certainly discourage students from participating in is called *iki, iki* where students are goaded into drinking their entire drinks in one gulp—a sure way to get drunk really fast to a point of no return.

Remarkably, though, with the high number of really inebriated people stumbling about, everyone is quite orderly and fisticuffs are actually quite rare. Normally, the various groups take good care of those who are in their charge, making sure they get home in one piece.

The custom of cherry blossom viewing has a long history in Japan. During the Heian Period (from the 8th to the 12th centuries), *hanami* parties were very popular with upper-class society and the aristocracy. Eventually, the custom spread among the common people during the Edo period (1568-1600) which still continues today.

Japan is a nation obsessed during this well-anticipated season. It is interesting to watch news reporters who are sent out to find the best viewing spots around Japan, interviewing people, and then reporting live on the status of the blossoms. Nightly newscasts show the gradual progression of the flowering blossoms each day by delicately shading a map of Japan in pink indicating where the blossoms have begun to flower.

The blossoms come and go in the south of Japan, well before they are about to bloom in the northern-most part of the country. Luckily for me, the city where I live—Hirosaki—boasts one of the most spectacular cherry blossom festivals in the country. People from all over Japan make their way here every year to stroll through the park where Hirosaki Castle is located, to enjoy this once a year spectacle just as the *samurai* of yesteryear did. Literally, there are thousands of cherry trees around this medieval castle and moat that are as old as the castle itself.

Several years ago, the blossom viewing had an added treat for me. After years of describing in minute detail this most unique and wonderful attraction, an old and dear friend finally made the long trek from home to my little corner of the world in order to see for herself this most splendid display of Mother Nature. As we leisurely strolled through the many pathways lined with trees in full bloom, she paused momentarily to gaze at the sea of pink flowers that made a canopy-like tunnel over our heads that extended for what seemed like an eternity. She said, "You know, there are no words to accurately describe what we are seeing. It's beyond beautiful." All I could say was, "I told you so."

[21] *Christmas in Japan*

Celebrating Christmas in Japan is, at best, surreal for an outsider coming into the culture. Please do not misunderstand me—it is quite festive and contains all the affectations, embellishments, and gewgaws we have back home. But behind all of the glitz and glitter of the holiday, the actual reason for celebrating the season is noticeably absent here. For the most part, Christmas in Japan is strictly a secular, commercial enterprise nurtured by department stores and shops to increase sales during the winter season.

The notion of "Christmas" in Japan, however, is not a new concept but has a long history dating back to the mid-16th century when Spanish and Portuguese traders and missionaries first introduced the holiday. Once Japan opened up to the West during the Meiji Period (1868-1912), Christmas was more widely celebrated, but largely only among the small percentage of converted Christians in churches and schools that were founded by Christian missionaries. In the 1930s, department stores began to promote actively Christmas by having big sales; fortunately, the holiday coincided with the Japanese custom of doling out "year-end bonuses" giving consumers great purchasing power. Also, the Japanese custom of *seibo* (yearend presents) made the timing perfect to further exploit the commercial aspect of the season.

The difference between the celebrations held here and those held in other parts of the world have to do with the religious meaning and symbolism of the holiday. Since Japan is an overwhelmingly *Shinto* and Buddhist country, with only a very small minority of its people being practicing Christians, the celebration is less focused on the birth of Jesus and more centered on Santa Claus, Christmas trees, and the gift exchange aspect of the holiday.

Once I saw a rather curious representation of Christmas that could even be interpreted as disturbing—innocently done, I am convinced—but it illustrated to me just how unaware and confused most Japanese are regarding the origins of this adopted holiday. A store in Tokyo had gone to great lengths to decorate for the Christmas holiday, and as a centerpiece for the display, the designer had placed a huge lighted cross. Upon closer inspection, though, I was shocked to see a bearded Santa in the typical red suit hanging on the cross (a la Jesus in the Crucifixion).

I am sure that the creator of this display wanted to incorporate an element of Christianity into the overall design, but did not have enough knowledge or experience with Christmas to know what was appropriate. Likely, the person remembered that the holiday had something to do with Jesus, and had perhaps seen a cross with an individual hanging on it, but somehow confused the symbols for Easter with Christmas, mistakenly switching Jesus, a religious figure, with Santa, a pop culture icon. A huge gaffe, for sure, but probably not maliciously done as a statement against Christianity: just a cultural collision of pop culture and religious symbols.

Of course in predominantly Christian countries, riots and protests would ensue, with shoppers picketing and boycotting the store. In Japan, without the Christian tradition, background, and influence, people hardly paid it any attention at all other than to admire it as just another decorated Christmas display.

An unusual Christmas-related custom in Japan is to eat a bucket of Kentucky Fried Chicken on Christmas Eve. It is amazing how many families preorder and eat KFC on Christmas Eve night in Japan. Most likely, a very astute marketing executive for Japan's KFC headquarters started this yearly tradition of eating a bucket of chicken on Christmas

Eve via an aggressive (and obviously successful) advertising campaign when KFC first came to Japan. People order their buckets weeks in advance and line up on the evening of December 24th to pick them up. A friend told me that Japanese people associate eating turkey with the American celebration of Christmas, and since turkey is hard to come by here, the next best thing is chicken from an American restaurant.

Another widely practiced Japanese Christmas custom is the tradition of eating "Christmas Cake" on Christmas Eve. People order their cakes weeks in advance of the day, and at great expense. The average cake costs between $25-40 and is adorned with Christmas-related figurines and candles. The most popular cake ordered each year is a strawberry flavored sponge cake with thick, creamy vanilla icing. It best resembles a Western-style birthday cake but is much smaller (usually the circumference of a normal sized salad plate).

My students are always surprised to learn that this custom is 100% Japanese. They cannot believe that I grew up without ritualistically eating Christmas cake each year on Christmas Eve. This is definitely a kid's tradition here, and could be loosely compared to the custom of adults in a number of Western countries eating fruit cake during the holiday season. I do not know of any kids that like fruit cake, but all Japanese kids love Christmas cake.

When I first arrived in Japan back in the late 80s, there was a rather derogatory term used toward unmarried women that is related to the custom of eating Christmas cake. Women who were still unmarried at the age of 26 were referred to as being "Christmas cake." The idea was that no man would want to marry a woman who had passed her "25th" birthday, referencing December 25th—meaning no one wants to eat "Christmas cake" after the 25th of December.

A Kentucky Colonel statue dressed as Santa to entice patrons to order their chicken for Christmas Eve at KFC

Thankfully, I have not heard anyone use this unflattering term for quite some time. Today, it is common practice for men and women to marry later, in their late twenties, early thirties, or even older. The modern Japanese woman has become much more independent and self-sufficient, having many more options in her career and single life than her mother or grandmother ever had.

[22] *Year End Parties in Japan Celebrate "Forgetting" the Year*

Every year, throughout the month of December, a very important ritual is observed all over Japan—*bonenkai* (the year end party). Literally, the term *bonenkai* means "forget the year party," where colleagues and staff in companies, factories, schools—and just about any other group of people who are in regular contact with one another (i.e., clubs, associations, and the like)—meet to have a chance to forget all of the problems and worries they encountered over the past year.

These Japanese-style banquets usually start out quite formally with the guests sitting in long rows (at tables low to the floor, on cushions called *zabuton*) looking serious and demure, attentively listening to the party emcee. The formal atmosphere is quickly transformed once the official toast is made, signaling the start of the party. The guests then loosen up and begin to partake in the endless bottles of beer that are brought to the tables, along with drinking copious amounts of wine, *sake*, and other alcoholic beverages. Before living in Japan, I had no idea the important role alcohol plays in social gatherings here. It is certainly the social lubricant that keeps working relationships well-oiled. Most everyone drinks at least some alcohol and many drink a lot.

In general terms, there is no real stigma about getting drunk and behaving poorly because of alcohol in Japan, unlike in the United States where people are offended because of someone's alcohol induced unruliness and rude behavior. People in Japan who are inebriated and display less-than-polite behavior are readily forgiven by those in attendance because it is conventionally understood that it was the "alcohol" that caused the rude behavior or offhanded remarks. Rarely are drunkards held strictly accountable for their actions. Over the years, I have witnessed some rather bawdy conduct at some of these gatherings and usually the next day not a word of what occurred the previous night is mentioned. All is seemingly forgiven and largely forgotten.

Perhaps as a form of "stress release" is the primary reason that people (especially men) drink regularly. It is a way to relax after a hard day's work and it is a socially rooted custom that dates back centuries. It is during these times of "nomunication" (a coined word which takes the Japanese word for "drinking" and combines it with the English word for "communication") that one gets a glimpse of Japanese people's true colors—outside of the shackles of office protocol and societal obligation. The shyest of people, who never make spectacles of themselves at work or in public, are much less inhibited after a few drinks to get up and belt out a *karaoke* song or do a dance…or to state their true opinions about those around them. It is during these times that Japanese people feel they can be truly open and honest. If their honesty is too candid (i.e. offensive) with a supervisor or a colleague during one of these soirees, then all is forgiven the next morning and is blamed upon the alcohol.

Hamming it up at a *Bonenkai* (year end party) to the delight of colleagues and guests

The meals at these banquets often consist of a number of courses that arrive throughout the evening. Later, some type of entertainment is often offered during the meal, either by professional musicians or by some of the younger staff members who are relegated to regale everyone with a game, skit, or performance. In addition, bingo and *karaoke* seem to be favorites at these kinds of gatherings.

The initial formality is gradually replaced with loud laughter, sprinkled with lively and boisterous exchanges between workmates, impromptu singing, occasional dancing, and as the night wears on... some rather raucous (if not risqué and even bawdy) behavior by some of the more inebriated participants. These yearend parties give the normally subdued Japanese worker, or "salaryman," a chance to let loose and have a rip-roaring good time. I have attended parties where the shyest and most modest of my Japanese colleagues would transform themselves into party animals that at first shocked me, and then caused me to view them with befuddled amusement.

When I first arrived in Japan, my initial observations of my Japanese colleagues were in a largely work-only environment; this all changed when I got a glimpse of their true characters during my first *bonenkai* party held by the Board of Education office where I worked as a junior high school teacher. It was there that the normally humorless rank and file let down their guards, transfiguring their stoic and sober work-personas into fun loving and jovial pranksters who were extremely entertaining to be around.

My first clue that something big was about to happen, however, was the nearly giddy anticipation everyone exhibited leading up to the party day. An inordinate amount of planning and preparation had been going on for weeks. This was interesting to me, because it was all consuming and even bordered on being obsessive. These tasks fell to the youngest members of the office who were in charge of planning the big event. Our office did not merely have a "party" but we made it into a weekend event, staying overnight at a typical Japanese inn nestled in the mountains that featured a natural hot-spring bath.

On the day of the party, we left work early, taking a chartered bus to the venue. We quickly checked in (six people to a room, assigned by sex and age—the younger employees bunked together, the older ones together, with the men separated from the women) and immediately scurried off to the communal bath to relax before dinner. After bathing in scalding hot water, everyone then changed into *yukata*, a Japanese *kimono*-like garment supplied by the hotel, before going to the private dining room where the party was held.

Unbeknownst to me, I was part of the entertainment on this particular evening. Prior to the year-end party, there was an office pool where we had to rank the autumn *sumo* wrestlers according to who we thought would win. Having no idea who any of the famous or skillful wrestlers were, I randomly selected several not knowing what I was doing. Lo and behold, I won the office pool making me the *yokozuna* or "Grand Champion *Sumo* Wrestler." Part of the prize was the unique opportunity to wear an authentic *sumo* wrestling apron that featured elaborate hand embroidered scenes in silk. The two runner-ups also participated in this honor.

I had no idea what I would be expected to do, but luckily I had seen a *yokozuna* ceremony on TV where the wrestler, with great skill, moved his arms and legs in precise movements. I, of course, faked it. At first, I was somewhat credible, but the fact that I was wearing an "Indiana" sweatshirt and matching Santa hat detracted from the seriousness of trying to do it convincingly well. It was all in good fun, though, and I gladly hammed it up to everyone's delight.

I always look forward to these yearly soirees because it is an opportunity to witness a side of my colleagues that I rarely get a chance to see within the confines of our professional relationship. Of course, no matter how crazy or boorish someone might have behaved during the *bonenkai*, all is usually forgiven the next day and the subject is never broached except to say how enjoyable the entire event was.

The majority of Japanese take the position of why stir up bad feelings over something that was said or done when under the influence of alcohol when it is the day-to-day relationship that really matters? A cultural pill that is sometimes hard to swallow for someone coming in from outside the culture.

Part IV:

Political, Educational and Social Issues

[23] *Immigration and Japan*

Until a number of years ago, it was quite rare for foreigners to go through the actual immigration process where they take Japanese citizenship, making them, in essence, Japanese. Traditionally, the majority of expatriates that decided to call Japan home were people who chose to come here for professional reasons and were quite happy to glide back and forth between Japan and their home countries, being satisfied with a "work visa" or "permanent residency."

Previously, I used to have a three-year "professor's visa" until I applied and received "permanent residency." This allows me to come back and forth to Japan freely and to stay and work legally for as long as I wish. It is not Japanese citizenship, but a long-term visa that allows me more freedom to live and work here, similar to an American "green card" that resident aliens are granted who reside in the US for an extended period of time.

The proverbial "bubble" economy that Japan enjoyed in the 1980s made it necessary to loosen the restrictions regarding "visiting workers" giving them a new status. A shortage of laborers during that time period required Japan to open its borders to allow laborers and unskilled workers to do the jobs that many Japanese people refused to do.

This is similar to the situation in the United States where migrant workers from Mexico were needed to pick produce during the summer and autumn seasons in the upper Midwest, and in Florida and California during the winter and spring seasons. Many of these workers, after years of working and residing in the United States, opted to make the US their home.

The original intention of the Japanese government, I believe, was that the migrant workers would come into Japan to shore up the labor shortage for a short-term stint, and then return to their home countries with money in their pockets and hopefully some new job skills that they could then use there. What the government did not count on was that many of these people who came from countries where the economies were not doing as well, had political strife, or were at war, decided to stay in Japan. Some of these workers married Japanese nationals, had children, and set up house. Others lived illegally, continuing to do the jobs that no one else wanted to do. The government officials largely turned a blind eye to such practices because a need was being filled.

Fast forward a couple of decades and now there are communities in the larger cities where pockets of foreign nationals live together creating entire neighborhoods of non-Japanese from the same ethnic background. No concrete programs were ever introduced to help these people assimilate, so there are instances where problems have arisen where the foreign workers have not adapted well to Japanese culture, and are now being shunned in Japanese mainstream communities by the locals.

This only exacerbates the situation because instead of trying to assist these newcomers to Japan to live and work alongside their Japanese counterparts, little ghettos are being created where these foreigners become isolated, making their Japanese neighbors suspicious of their ways of living, which fuels the tendency of mainstream Japanese to become insular in their thinking toward these newcomers.

A good example of this dates back to the late 1980s when a town in the southern prefecture of Aichi, Homigaoka, desperately needed workers to fill a severe labor shortage. The town officials thought a solution would be to employ ethnic Japanese-Brazilians. Physically they looked Japanese, even having Japanese surnames. Ethnically and culturally, however, they were 100% Brazilian. Their grandparents had emigrated from Japan to Brazil in search of a better life. Probably the first generation after the initial wave of immigrants lived a largely Japanese life in Brazil. Each ensuing generation, however, became more Brazilian until the 1980s when the large majority of the Japanese-Brazilians who, like their great-grandparents before them who were searching for a better life, came back to Japan to find work.

First Japanese immigrants in Brazil, aboard Kasato Maru ship in port of Santos, Brazil[3]

The Japanese government created a new type of working visa to allow these second and third generation Japanese-Brazilians to work in Japan more easily (cutting out much of the bureaucratic red tape normally required to work in Japan). The problem was, though, they were so far removed from their Japanese roots that they readily identified with their Brazilian culture and traditions more so than their Japanese ethnic heritage. Nearly all of them had no real Japanese language skills, had not eaten Japanese food prior to coming to Japan, and had no idea about Japanese etiquette, traditions or culture. The town officials assumed because they "looked" Japanese, that they would "behave" like Japanese. With no programs in place to assist these newly arrived immigrants to fit into their new surroundings and life, problems soon arose with mainstream Japanese who found themselves sharing their community with the Brazilians.

I remember a newspaper article during this time that listed all the improper things the Brazilians were doing that horrified the local native Japanese population. One of the biggest offenses to the locals was that some of the Brazilians would go to the local public bath wearing swimming trunks—treating it more like a "hot tub" than the intended "bath tub."

Few people here can deny the economical impact the cheap labor has had on Japan's auto industry, making it quite competitive on the world market. This is the short-term gain companies enjoyed by employing so many foreign workers in the "just in time" auto manufacturing system. This system allows for a lower overhead because instead of having all the components made in one location, companies like Toyota subcontract much of the production to smaller companies that are very dependent upon the cheap labor that the Brazilian-Japanese immigrants offer. Each component is delivered "just in time" on the assembly line which cuts down on the size of factories and the need to stock so many parts.

The downside to this is that these workers, many which now have permanent residency and can stay in Japan indefinitely, are officially categorized as only being "part-time" workers (even though they work a 40 hour or more week), which means that companies do not have to pay higher wages, or pay into the health-insurance or pension fund schemes for these employees, leaving many without proper healthcare and no real retirement plan in place. In the long-term, by saving money now by not paying the workers sufficient incomes, and by not insisting they have proper socialized health insurance and retirement benefits, what will happen to these people when they have debilitating, chronic illnesses or when they are elderly?

These questions have not been fully answered by Japanese government officials. For the time-being they are like ostriches with their heads in the sand pretending all is well. The next couple of decades will see huge demographic changes in Japan when the children of the immigrants begin to marry and have families, changing the entire landscape of Japan. Before this occurs, however, a more serious problem is plaguing the offspring of these newcomers: education.

There is no law that requires compulsory education of the children of these immigrants in Japan. Although the majority does attend school, the dropout rate is high because there are no systematic programs in place to teach Japanese as a Second Language (JSL) to these immigrant children, so their written Japanese and ability to function in mainstream Japanese schools are weak. It is difficult enough for native Japanese children to keep up with all the *kanji* (Chinese) characters they must learn each year to be able to read and write properly. It is doubly difficult for children who are basically thrown into a mainstream classroom with no remedial assistance or special tutoring.

The future social implications of this are tremendous. Without proper education and know-how, which would allow these children to have some semblance of social mobility once they become adults, will further cast them into a lower socio-economic bracket because they will not be able to perform any worthwhile jobs other than menial labor.

Japan is at a huge crossroads currently. The population of Japan is dangerously low which has caused elementary schools across the country to close, which is currently making universities jittery as this wave eventually will cause a goodly number of universities, colleges, junior colleges and trade-schools to either scale-back or close.

Japan's future, whether it wants to admit it or not, is going to be closely intertwined with a large migration of foreigners who will come to Japan for short-term work to fill the growing shortage of workers, but who will end up staying on permanently. These foreigners will then marry, have children, and become a part of the changing face of Japan. Will Japan embrace these people by offering them proper visas, insurance and pension schemes, as well as education, to make them more functional in society? Or will Japan use them for labor only, denying these workers equal rights and a proper livelihood, by casting them away when no longer needed?

It will be interesting to see which direction Japan takes. If past directives and attitudes are any indication, however, the future looks rather bleak for these immigrant workers who are hoping to call Japan home. The United States certainly has handled the immigration of workers to the US horribly which is why the 2008 presidential election focused on this issue until the economy took a turn for the worse, which then put illegal immigrants on the back burner temporarily. Japan may very well be having the same contentious debates that the United States is having in 20 years if it does not start accepting the harsh reality that in order for it to maintain its competitive edge and world standing, it will have to accept and assimilate immigrants into its society, offering these workers a way to live and work alongside Japanese people that gives them equal footing and personal dignity. Only time will tell.

[24] *A Week's Worth of News from Japan*

When outside of Japan, a common question I am asked is about "crime" in Japan. It seems people have heard about Japan's safe reputation and want to know if it is actually as "safe" as the propaganda would have one to believe. The answer is yes…and no. Comparatively, Japan can be regarded as a relatively safe country when comparing it to other industrialized countries. The crime rate is much lower for serious crimes, perhaps, but Japan has its fair share of "crime."

I decided a good way to get a sampling of the types of crimes committed in Japan would be to scan one week's worth of newspapers to cull and glean stories about crime. The *Daily Yomiuri* and *The Japan Times* are the two major English dailies that most foreigners living in Japan read regularly. Some of the stories I found are rather benign... others bordering on weird...while others quite heinous.

Japan, just like any other industrialized nation, has its share of social misfits. Of course, statistically the crime rate in Japan is one of the lowest in the world considering the number of people living on the Japanese archipelago. Generally, I feel quite safe to stroll at night in any part of my city, and even in Tokyo. There are random acts of violence that do occur, but they are rare. Such instances, however, do receive nationwide attention when they happen. So, for one week I clipped articles out of the national English dailies to get a pulse rate of what types of crimes were committed in that short time span.

First, I'll start with the more benign infractions. As with any country where there are politicians, a smattering of political "white collar" crimes was reported. Typical political scandals involving paybacks, embezzlement, and price fixing for kickbacks seem to be standard fodder in most societies, Japan being no different.

One instance involved a government worker who had embezzled one million yen (nearly $10,000) from a pension fund. This does not seem like a lot of money, but it could only be the tip of the iceberg. It seems that accounting practices have not been so thorough in many sectors of the government and the floodgates could very well open up exposing even more impropriety.

Perhaps the story here is that it made the national papers. In fact, because crime is so much lower in Japan, things that might only get a small blurb in a local newspaper in other countries will get front page, headline coverage here. The pension fund, however, has become especially vulnerable to theft which has everyone very nervous here. With the ever-aging population, along with the decrease in population of young people, keeping the pension fund solvent for the long-term may prove to be very tricky indeed. A scandal involving the government losing millions of data entries of paid premiums from the early 70s has people up in arms and demanding that their monthly checks be reevaluated to make sure they are receiving the proper amount of social security.

Rarely is there not some article or news brief each week detailing Japanese politicians' antics, usually bumbling remarks and verbal gaffes that have gotten them into hot water due to racist or discriminatory comments. There have been a parade of politicians over the years—too many to count—who have fallen from power in disgrace from scandals involving the usual reasons that such things happen: graft, corruption, extramarital affairs, etc.

Moving on to more serious things, a headline on the second page of the newspaper read "Son arrested for alleged neglect of elderly mom." A 53-year-old man was arrested for abandoning his mother in their home who was bedridden. When arrested he only offered the reason, "I was tired of taking care of my mother." An astute neighbor noticed no one coming and going from the house for a week and alerted authorities.

Government issued pension books[4]

As terrible as it is, I am afraid that many people in other countries have become insensitive to such crimes because of their frequency. I doubt that a national newspaper—or even a statewide publication—would necessarily pick this story up. It would remain news only to the community in which it happened.

Another full-fledged scandal involving possible murder (that is rocking Japan's revered *Sumo* world to its very core) involved a hazing incident that went terribly wrong. A junior wrestler was mercilessly beaten by his seniors and, of all people, the stable master—who is in charge of making sure he is well-taken care of and trained properly.

The stable master, a surly acting and looking fellow, Tokitsukaze, admitted hitting the teenager in the head with a beer bottle the day before, and allowing other wrestlers to beat him with a metal bat by saying, "You can teach him a lesson, too."—unbelievable, indeed.

It is astonishing that the stable master, a professional "teacher" who is charged with the responsibility of caring for and training these future wrestlers would be so callous and indifferent towards a boy in his charge. The stable master, after the boy collapsed the next day, waited several hours to call an ambulance, telling the other wrestlers not to go near the boy. It was reported his body was covered with bruises, abrasions and burn marks.

Needless to say, this has caused quite a furor here, wreaking havoc on an already tainted sport that is teetering from accusations of bout-fixing, and the faking of injuries by a top-ranked wrestler—Mongolian superstar, Ashashoryu, in order to have an extended vacation to his homeland—among other, smaller infractions too numerous to mention here.

The most heart wrenching part about this story was the enormous guilt the boy's father felt afterwards. It seems his son had called a number of times wanting to quit and come home because of the brutality at the hands of the boy's teammates, but the father thought it was not so serious and encouraged him to continue and tough it out.

Of course, the boy probably did not tell his father the whole story about how severe his beatings had become. After all, it is quite an honor to be accepted into a *sumo* stable to train in Japan. Entire communities rally around their homegrown wrestlers, encouraging them to do their best. Besides, hazing of junior wrestlers by their seniors is a well-established part of the severe "training" they receive.

The teenage wrestler did attempt to run away on several occasions only to have his teammates catch him to drag him back. When all of this occurred, it took several months before news of it only leaked out.

Obviously, there was an attempt to cover things up by the *sumo* stable where the boy died. In fact, the stable master offered to have the boy's body cremated and the ashes sent to the parents. The parents resisted and pushed for an autopsy as for a cause of death (which was originally recorded as being a "heart attack").

In the more heinous category of crimes, a university student in Kagawa Prefecture was arrested for raping a woman that resulted in injury. Now they are suspecting that he may be involved in as many as ten unsolved rapes in the area. Again, this type of crime would probably not receive such widespread attention in most countries, but since a suspect was apprehended, it made national news here.

There was a rash of suicides that occurred as well during the week I collected stories for this essay. These were actually much more numerous than what was officially reported. This is one aspect where Japanese people have become a bit desensitized because of the frequency.

One, however, was a 16-year-old boy which seems to be a trend that is quite common among young people after summer vacations and right after winter vacations. The details of this student's suicide were not stated, but most likely it had to do with bullying which is a national problem and a stain on Japan's educational system. Suicide in Japan does not have the same taboo it does in Christian-Judeo based societies. Sometimes it is a way to save face in order to avoid public humiliation.

On the same day, it was reported that an executive for the winter sport of curling was found hanged in a forest in Hokkaido. It seems that in March he resigned from an auditing committee in his village after allegedly burning receipts totaling millions of yen when he served as deputy mayor of the small village. In a way, his decision to commit suicide effectively demonstrated his shame for the situation and that he took responsibility for his actions. It is hard to understand this logic for people not raised in a culture where such actions are not necessarily looked down upon, but often are viewed as being dignified in some way.

In the category of just plain weird, a man was indicted for stalking a woman to whom he had attached a Global Positioning System (GPS) device to her car so he could track her whereabouts at all times. Using it to follow her, he was reported to have checked her position on "several thousand occasions." Can we say obsessive? That was one busy man. The victim became suspicious, however, when he happened to show up at a place where she normally would not have gone, but yet he coincidentally was there. This ended on a good note, with him being taken into custody without any harm being done to her, except for probably finding the whole saga quite creepy and invasive.

A vice principal of a middle school was held over the undressing of an intoxicated woman who had fallen asleep in a pub. He allegedly removed her panties to photograph her with his cell phone. Unfortunately, misbehaving teachers is an all too common news story in Japan of late. Usually it involves improper acts of a male teacher with an underage female student. This week, though a twist on this type of story occurred that mirrors the sensational case in the United States involving Mary Kay Le Tourneau some years back.

A distraught husband called to report his wife (and mother of three) missing after five days. The 42-year-old middle school music teacher had started an affair with a former student who was only 16-years-old. They were caught at a police checkpoint after living it up at resort hotels during the duration. The officers reported that when apprehended she had a vacant look on her face and admitted the affair had been going on since March. The age of consensual sex in Japan is 18-years-old.

Finally, one story that caught my eye, that is not a crime, per se, but certainly bizarre is about a 60-year-old single woman who was impregnated with an egg from the United States. The immediate problem was trying to find a doctor and hospital to take her on as a patient. Generally, obstetricians are, as a rule, prohibited from assisting with births involving donated embryos. The main concern, other than the obvious risks to the mother having a child at such an advanced age, is the future of the child. Since she is single, chances are her parents are quite elderly, so if something should happen to her, what would happen to the child? In such a case, adopting an older child would have been more prudent I think. This, unfortunately, is not a viable option for many couples and single people in Japan as people and society in general has an aversion to accepting children adopted from a different family or bloodline.

[25] *Adoption in Japan*

Adoption in Japan is something that is quite rare, and when it does happen, the parents often do all they can to keep this fact a secret from neighbors and friends.

When I first came to Japan to live permanently in the late 80s, there was a staff member who worked in my office as a driver. He and his wife were young, energetic and a lot of fun. In other words, they were potentially ideal parents.

Once when we were discussing marriage and family, they admitted to me that they were not able to have children of their own, and although saddened by this, they had accepted that they would always be childless. Being a naïve twenty-something, I immediately suggested that they adopt a child from one of the many orphanages that are located all over Japan. They both looked at me as if I had a horn growing out of my head.

Quickly, the husband said it was not an option, while his wife nodded in agreement. I was puzzled as to why, so I pressed them to explain their reasoning further. It seems that although they personally were not opposed to adopting a child from another family as their own, their families would be dead-set against it.

In Japan, many people have a rather deep-seated aversion to adoption, placing greater importance on blood relations. Often when a child is rendered parentless within a family, for whatever reasons, the extended family of the child will often take the child to rear through adulthood. If this is not an option, then many families would prefer the child be placed in a government run home—orphanage—rather than to allow complete strangers to adopt the child.

The childless couple who was telling me all of this also said that they worried that their families would not accept an adopted child the same way they would a biological child. Besides, they were afraid of what might happen to the child at school by classmates and teachers if it were ever found out the child was not their own, or how neighbors would treat them if the truth were ever found out.

Of course, this example is nearly 20-years-old, and perhaps Japanese society has evolved a bit with all of the internationally reported adoptions of Hollywood stars like Mia Farrow, Rosie O'Donnell, Madonna, and Angelina and Brad Jolie-Pitt.

So, I decided to present this question to my fourth year "Cross-Cultural Studies Seminar" class recently. I first presented the topic by reviewing the high-profile adoptions in recent years; and the trend in the United States for couples to travel to Asia (i.e. China or Korea) or to Central America (i.e. Guatemala) to adopt orphaned children. I also related to them that in my family I have four adopted cousins who were a very important part of my life while growing up.

My students were surprised that many American couples opted to adopt children from different ethnic backgrounds or races. I explained that a "child is a child" and many American couples just want to experience the joy of having a child, so the child's ethnic background is often not an issue when deciding to adopt from a foreign country.

I then asked the students how they felt about adoption after this short presentation. It was interesting that nearly all of my Japanese students felt that it was a good thing for people to adopt children, and it was better for a child to be in a loving home rather than to be in an orphanage. Curiously, though, when I asked if any of them would consider adopting a child, not one said they would. I changed the dynamic of the question by asking that if for some reason they could not have a biological child of their own, would they then consider adopting a child from another family?

Again, no one felt that they would ever be able to do that, offering as reasons much of what I mentioned earlier—extended family concerns about accepting the child fully into the family, society's attitude toward the child, potential bullying at school, and an additional reason, worrying that the personality of the child would not fit that of a child that was a biological son or daughter. Obviously, not much has changed in twenty years because the attitude in my small, unscientific study seems to mirror what has been traditionally the attitude in Japan toward adoption.

A foreign friend of mine and his Japanese wife has two biological sons. The oldest son befriended a boy in high school who had lived in an orphanage his entire life. When the boy turned 18-years-old, he had to leave the facility and basically had no place to go. My friend's son asked his parents if he could come to their home for a bit until he could get used to living outside the orphanage, get some job-training, and find employment. They, of course, agreed and the boy came to live with them.

What was most noticeable about the boy was the fact that he had not really ever had any "family-based" experiences. He had always been in the facility and never did normal family things. For instance, they said that he ate absolutely everything on his plate, no matter what. This was an orphanage rule—to eat every bit of what is given to you whether you like it or not. Also, he was completely silent during meals, another rule at the facility.

They purchased some clothes for him and he started to write his name on the label, which was necessary in the orphanage. He had his own room in their home, which made him uncomfortable because he was used to being in a room full of people at night. Soon after he arrived to their home, my friends learned it was his birthday so they prepared a birthday cake with candles as a surprise. The boy was so touched that he cried because he had never had, nor seen, a birthday cake.

As is typical in most families, they would order pizza on some nights when they did not want to cook. He had never experienced eating carry-out food as a family—eating what and how much he wanted. Needless to say, it broke their hearts to think he had not experienced many of the ordinary things that most families take for granted. He eventually was able to relocate to Tokyo where he is training as an apprentice in a *sushi* shop, learning a trade that will make him a productive, self-sufficient member of Japanese society.

The reasons children end up in government run orphanages in Japan mirror why American children end up in foster care—the parents are deceased, the children were abandoned, abused or neglected by their caretakers. Seldom do people in Japan discuss orphaned children, making them almost invisible to society because they are kept behind closed doors. There is definitely a stigma attached to a child who has grown up in an orphanage, making it difficult when they are placed into mainstream society to find proper work, housing, and to form lasting relationships with others. Many Japanese families, I am sure, would not be so keen to have a child marry a person who grew up in an orphanage due to the societal attitude toward such people, in a country where appearance is everything and image by others is taken very seriously.

This is probably where my personal cultural bias moves in, coming from a society and culture where it is believed that children are better off in "foster care" with families who are vetted and willing to accept the child into their home. The sterile and cold surroundings of a facility, in my logic, must be far worse than being placed in a family home. Perhaps such a system of foster care would never work in Japan due to the aversion of caring for a stranger's child. If adoption is viewed so gloomily in Japan, I am sure the same issues and problems surrounding a family who wanted to adopt would be the same for a family who wanted to foster a child.

I have had so many opportunities in my life to travel and see the world. One thing I often tried to do on these trips was to visit orphanages in the countries I visited. When I lived in Costa Rica, I visited a number of times an orphanage near my home with a couple of friends from Nicaragua. When I asked the caretaker at the orphanage what I could do, she just said "please hold as many babies as you can... they need human contact." I did and although it was seemingly a small contribution, it was powerfully moving for me.

To think that by merely cradling a baby can make a difference in that child's life taught me something very valuable: Never underestimate the power of a simple act of kindness. It was not the act of giving so much, but it was what I received in return—the feeling of having done something of use for a fellow being who, at that moment, most needed something as easy as a caring touch.

A few years ago, a Catholic-run hospital in Kumamoto City, in southern Japan, caused a nationwide conundrum when they opened Japan's first "baby hatch" where parents could drop off unwanted babies—no questions asked. The baby hatch is basically an incubator that is accessible from outside through a hinged door. Once a baby is placed inside, an alarm alerts the hospital staff to go immediately to fetch the baby.

One of the first children left there was a 3-year-old who was able to tell the nurses and doctors that his "daddy" left him there. Other babies, some just hours old, have been left since the hatch became available. There are many critics to this baby drop-off system who maintain it will encourage parents who no longer want to take responsibility for their children basically to abandon them. Supporters say that it will save the lives of children who are at risk due to neglect or abuse by parents who cannot cope emotionally, afford to raise, or who do not really want them to begin with. The babies who are abandoned in the hatch most likely will be placed in government facilities and the chances of them being adopted are slim because of the aversion to adoption Japanese society has.

The former Prime Minister, Shinzo Abe, who resigned only after a year due to scandals that plagued his administration, was a vocal opponent of the baby hatch when it first opened stating it encouraged parents not to be responsible for their duties. It should be noted that he and his wife, Akie, are childless and went public with their fertility issues; it was reported that Mr. Abe had suggested adoption to his wife, but Mrs. Abe publicly rejected the notion of adopting a child, stating "I could not accept this and was not confident about bringing up an adoptee properly, so it did not happen."

It is reported that there are some 30,000 Japanese children living in government facilities. When a child is considered for adoption, it is not uncommon for the legal guardian or next of kin to reject the application, opting for the child to stay in the orphanage instead. There is a longing, perhaps, by these people that someday the parents who abandoned the child will return, or financially an extended family member may be able to afford to take the child, or the abusive or neglectful parent will reform and be able to once again care for the child.

Unfortunately, these cases are quite rare and the child ends up spending his/her entire adolescent life until adulthood in the facility. It is almost an attitude that if children cannot live with the parents then it is somehow better for them to live in an institution rather than to be adopted out to an unrelated-by-blood family.

One issue that has arisen regarding the legality of the baby hatch is that once a baby is left there, it is up to the courts to rule the baby officially "abandoned" or the baby could theoretically be left in an orphanage its entire life because of the possibility the parents may come back someday to pick the child up.

The Japanese system of *koseki* which legally records such life events as marriages, births, and deaths in a family registry traditionally viewed adoption or divorce as being blemishes upon the family name. In the late 1980s, the law changed which made it possible for adopted children to have their birth name changed officially to the adopted family name. Before, both names were registered which basically served as a neon sign saying ADOPTED.

Prior to the change in the law, it was easy for adopted children to be discriminated against in many parts of society. Still, it is difficult for children who grew up in children's homes to get a fair shake when it comes to receiving higher education, securing employment, and being emotionally stable enough to get involved in relationships.

Orphaned children are guaranteed a safe place to live, food, clothing, and education through high school. Once they become adults, they are basically on their own and if they want to attend university, they must pay for it themselves. Needless to say, these kids normally do not have the resources to pay for college tuition, so a large percentage does not go on to university.

Families who do adopt will sometimes move immediately to a place where they are not known in order to avoid the prying eyes of people who may look down upon adoption. This is to avoid any potential problems or societal prejudices the couple may face by outsiders. These couples also have to deal with unsympathetic family members who may oppose the adoption because the child is not related by blood.

Curiously, it is common in Japan for an elderly couple, or older single woman, to adopt a son for inheritance purposes. This seems to be acceptable by society, but usually the adopted "child" is an adult and it is done for legal reasons to carry on a family name, etc.

The aversion to adoption in Japan may have its roots in Confucian ideas that came from China and Korea more than a millennium ago where reverence to parents and the relationship between parents and children was paramount in the smooth functioning of society. The belief in ancestral worship is an important part of Buddhism, also, which perhaps helped to perpetuate the belief in the idea of "pure" and "impure" blood within families and groups of people. This makes a recognizable bloodline important for religious reasons.

Coming from a culture where adoption is completely accepted and embraced, it is sometimes difficult for me to understand what all the fuss is about in Japan regarding adoption. Why deny parents and children the opportunity to become a family? It is a win-win situation for the childless parents who desperately want a child...and for the child who would benefit from having a real family and home life to grow up in.

Japan has certainly experienced some far reaching social changes in the last few decades: allowing women to become professionals who sometimes choose to forego motherhood for careers; or where young people have increasingly been rejecting the stodgy customs of their elders for more personal freedom and independence, causing the older generation to wring their hands with concern; and changing from a nation that had families caring for their old people, going from having few nursing home-like facilities, to having many such facilities with fewer older people living with their children.

Only time will tell, but there may come a time in the not so distant future where adoption will be embraced by younger generations. Just like past traditions being cast aside for more modern ones, the older generation will just have to deal with it.

[26] *Net Café Refugees*

A recent phenomenon in Japan that has the Ministry of Health, Labor, and Welfare troubled and ill at ease is a social trend that is occurring regarding young people and housing. A growing number of young people are what the media are labeling "Net Café Refugees"—basically people who have no place to live; have no regular employment but want to work; and who mostly work as "day" laborers or temp staff (being hired by the day or week).

The Net Cafés began to notice regulars who would come and stay for extended periods starting a couple of years ago. They would arrive, rent a spot, and stay the night. Many Net Cafés have individual cubicles with desktop computers on a table with a chair that customers can use for as long as they wish.

Once this trend of people staying started to become the norm, many Net Cafés began to sell food, offer more comfortable recliner-style chairs, and even provide a place to take a shower for an additional fee. The cost to stay in one of these cubicles range from $7 - $15 per night, which is much cheaper than the cheapest hotel (including the much publicized "capsule hotels" that many businesspeople use—essentially a pod with a bed and TV).

Originally, these Net Cafés were *manga kissa* (comic book coffee shops) where people could go for a cup of coffee and spend endless hours reading through the collection of comic books the shop had on display. These eventually modernized to include computers, becoming Net Cafés offering customers semi-private spaces where they can surf the Net for hours on end. It was not long until those people who had no place to call home saw these shops as an opportunity to be in a warm, clean place for the night...and for a nominal fee. There are just under

3,000 Net Cafés all around Japan, and it was reported recently that somewhere around 75% of these had "Net Café Refugees"—people who basically live from day-to-day in these cafés.

The reasons why people find themselves "homeless"—for lack of a better term—are many and varied. One real problem is that when the bubble burst in the early 1990s, companies were allowed to get away with hiring people as "part-timers" even though they may work a full 40-hour week. By labeling these workers as being only part-time, the employer was not legally required to offer the worker the normal perks that tenured workers enjoy (i.e. two yearly bonuses, health insurance, pensions, etc.). The companies did indeed save money, but the result is a generation of young people who basically are largely unskilled and too old to be considered for full-time work by many companies who actively and assertively practice age discrimination in hiring new recruits (preferring to hire fresh-out-of-college graduates now that the economy has started to turn-around).

These perpetual part-time workers have basically fallen through the cracks and are living hand to mouth for the most part. Renting an apartment is not an option because the initial cost to do so is so exorbitant in Japan that many cannot afford the two months' rent of "key money" (non-refundable money paid to the property owner to get the "key," which must be paid every two years on average) and the one to two months' rent as a deposit.

This is a huge chunk of change to have to provide up front, on top of the actual rent for the apartment that is required before moving into the abode. Full-time workers who are employed by big companies are often placed in subsidized housing or are given a percentage of their monthly rent which is paid by the company. "Freeters" or part-timers do not have this luxury.

Another group of people who use Net Cafés as their homes are workers who leave their hometowns to go to the bright lights of the big cities only to find it impossible to make any headway financially. A lack of employment opportunities most likely forced them to leave their hometowns only to find it as difficult to find regular employment in the big cities. So, they work in the day at odd jobs, making enough money for food and the fee to stay the night in the Net Café; the next morning they pay another small fee for a shower; and then put what little belongings they have in a train station locker before going out to find work for the day.

It is a vicious cycle that does not allow these types of people to ever really get ahead. They are constantly trying to make ends meet. Some of these people, of course, were thrown out of their childhood homes hence they cannot return to their parents' home for help. Others may not want to admit to their families that they are in such dire straits, worrying about losing face in front of their families by admitting their failure in not being able to make it on their own, hence choosing to live in these cafés.

Still, another group of people who live in these cafés are actual salaried workers but who live so far away from their workplace that it is more time-efficient for them to stay in Net Cafés, Monday through Friday, returning to their apartments or homes on the weekends. I personally know people who have several hours of daily commute by trains to and from their place of employment—leaving the house by 6:00 am and returning home after midnight. It is easy to see why some single people would opt to stay in a Net Café in order to get some much needed rest. Also, it has been reported that women who find themselves in abusive relationships will opt to stay in the Net Cafés to escape the spousal abuse they are enduring at home. Net Cafés offer a safe-haven for women who have no other place to go.

Since these cafés are open 24/7, people who find part-time work at night can arrive in the early morning and spend the day sleeping before heading back out to work again in the evening.

A worst case scenario are the people who cannot afford the fee to spend time at a Net Café but opt to go to an all night restaurant—they are called "Mac *Nannmin*" (or MacDonald's Refugee). For the cost of a cup of coffee, people are allowed to sit at a table and doze for the entire night.

I am sure that Mac Donald's does not encourage this, but a paying customer is a paying customer. In the United States, these types of customers would eventually be asked to leave due to loitering laws that prohibit such behavior. Sadly, this last step is truly one cup of coffee away from being "homeless" completely, and that, too, is a social problem that has become prevalent in Japan.

When I first arrived to live in Japan in the late 1980s, one question I inevitably was asked by people I first met was: "Why are there so many 'homeless' people in America?" This always put me on the defensive because it certainly was, and still is, a stain on the fabled American tapestry—one of the wealthiest nations in the world which prides itself at being a country based on personal freedom, the pursuit of happiness, and equal opportunity. I could never give a boxed answer that was satisfactory; there were many reasons, circumstances, and situations which caused people to find themselves homeless with no place to go.

When I worked in Washington, D.C. for the Governor of Indiana as a college intern, I had to walk to Capitol Hill from the place where I lived. Each day I passed through a park where homeless people gathered. What struck me at that impressionable age was how young all the homeless people looked to me. Why couldn't they work? Why didn't they have homes? To help answer these questions, I fortunately shared a house with a British aid worker who ran a soup kitchen to help feed the homeless who lived around Capitol Hill. On many occasions I volunteered to help serve food there on the weekends. It was an interesting experience, one that has stayed with me, making me appreciate having a home, food, family, friends, and everything that I want or need to be happy. My British roommate was selfless in his devotion to helping others and taught me some very valuable lessons about gratitude.

He also explained to me how some of these people ended up on the streets. Since this was the early 80s, many of the men were Vietnam vets who could not readjust to mainstream life after arriving back from the war nearly a decade before. Most all of the people—men and women—suffered from some sort of mental illness, and the majority were addicted to alcohol or drugs. For others, the reasons for the downward spiral had to do with bad financial investments where they lost everything, while others just decided to check out from dealing with the responsibilities of living in mainstream society. The majority of these reasons are in stark contrast to Japan's onslaught of homeless people.

The homeless problem in Japan did not begin until the proverbial economic bubble burst in the early 90s. Up to that point, homeless people virtually did not exist in Japan. Slowly, however, once the good times stopped rolling, many middle-aged men found themselves jobless, and in many cases, without family support. Men who found themselves homeless—sometimes out of shame, and in other instances, wives were fed up with out-of-work husbands and kicked them out—gravitated to large cities where they set up little tent cities in parks and under bridges.

The majority of homeless people in Japan are largely due to financial reasons, falling upon hard times. Interestingly, Japanese homeless people are not plagued by the mental illness, drug addiction and alcohol dependency that their American counterparts are. There are approximately 18,000 homeless people in Japan out of a population of around 127 million. Compare these numbers to that of the US which has 335,000 homeless with a total population of 300 million.

Japanese homeless people tend to maintain a sense of personal dignity while on the dole. Generally, they keep the area around their makeshift tents made out of plastic tarps and boxes quite orderly, clean and neat. In Tokyo, I often observe freshly washed shirts hanging on clotheslines outside their tents, as well as their shoes neatly lined up outside their shanties because to wear shoes inside one's home is culturally unacceptable here. Of course, there are the homeless people here who have no personal hygiene, are mentally ill, and who do have alcohol and drug problems—the percentages of these types, though, are much lower in comparison to North America and Europe.

There does seem to be a strong sense of community among the homeless in Japan. Many can be seen socializing with one another, as well as pitching in to keep the area where they live tidy and neat. They are quite self-sufficient, cooking meals on portable hot plates and using the somewhat clean public restrooms located in most Japanese parks to wash themselves, their dishes, and clothes.

There are less than 25 official shelters around Japan that are funded by the government. The numbers of homeless at any given time fluctuates with the economic condition—a robust economy has fewer homeless people while a bad economy forces more people onto the streets to live. Tokyo has tried to relocate a large percentage of homeless men by offering them job training and two years of government subsidized rent to help get them on their feet.

While riding the trains and subways around Tokyo, I have noticed homeless people scouring the cars for discarded magazines and comic books which they discount and resell on the street to make money. Usually these items are only slightly used, making their resale quite possible. Again, this has to do with self-sufficiency.

The large majority of homeless people, mostly men, probably would have become Net Café Refugees had such places existed when the economic bubble burst back in the early 90s. Today, young people who find themselves in the financial doldrums can maneuver about the cafés, maintaining a semblance of not being homeless, when in fact that is what they are. The only difference between the Net Café Refugee and the truly homeless person who lives under a bridge under tarps is circumstance. The social ills that caused the old-timers to live on the streets is nearly the same as those that now cause this younger generation to fall on hard times, living from hand to mouth in public spaces, not having any real place to call "home."

Curiously, after Japan's homeless problem became so prominent in the early 90s, I was never asked that question about America's homeless problem...funny how that works.

[27] *"Top-Heavy" Japan a Cause for Concern for Future Generations*

Japan has been experiencing, for a number of years, a very serious crisis: a declining population. The rapid demographic changes that are still occurring will have far-reaching and long-lasting repercussions on this country that will be felt for generations to come. Unfortunately, there seems to be no reversal in sight of this troubling trend, which is further serving to perplex Japan's leaders and academicians. It is a crisis that is unprecedented in the history of Japan.

For the first time in modern times, the number of babies born was fewer than people dying, meaning that the population is edging toward a configuration that makes it "top-heavy." The number of aged citizens is outpacing the number of babies being born. Experts are predicting that the declining number, which most likely will be in the tens of thousands in the next few years, will jump sharply into the hundreds of thousands by the time today's babies are adults. This is in a country that has one of the highest life expectancies in the world.

A briskly growing "graying" population, coupled with the sharp decrease in births, signals social and economic disaster in the future if drastic steps to remedy the situation are not taken immediately. The socialized health systems, as well as pensions for retirees, are at risk as the aging population drains the current funds with fewer future contributors on the horizon. As more and more Japanese continue to live well into their 80s, 90s and even 100s, the cost to care for these people will be put on the shoulders of today's young workers.

Adding to the immediacy of the situation is the fact that beginning in 2007, and continuing through 2009, the bulk of the World War

II Japanese "baby-boom" generation (who helped to fuel the system through their admirable work-ethic and prolific production of children) reached sixty—the general retirement age for Japanese workers. In the past, this system functioned smoothly because the number of deaths outpaced the number of new births, keeping the system "bottom-heavy." Why is Japan's population declining so rapidly?

There are a number of probable causes…from a sense of freedom afforded women to not only pursue careers, but to continue working well into their child-bearing years, to the high cost of raising a child from cradle until they are financially independent. There is no clear-cut reason as to why Japanese couples are opting to have less children (or none at all), but for sure it has been occurring for quite a while; the government certainly dropped the ball in trying to troubleshoot or reverse the trend at a time when it could have been corrected.

Hardest hit now are rural communities who are struggling to survive. Elementary schools are closing. Expectant mothers have a difficult time finding obstetricians because young doctors are opting to pursue residencies in fields that cater to the elderly. As well, young people are leaving in droves for the bright lights of the big cities. These communities are left to make do with an aging citizenry, with no influx of young blood in sight, to carry on with the farming or "Mom & Pop" type of shops and businesses that in the past were mainstays in rural Japan.

Traditionally, Japan has always been a "saving" nation which allowed retirees to enjoy a happy and somewhat carefree retirement. This has also changed in recent years due to the economic collapse of the bubble economy of the late 1980s and the migration of children to the big cities. In the past, children often returned to their hometowns after working a while in urban areas, but recently the trend has changed and many are not returning to care for their aged parents. Today, the elderly in Japan are spending more and more of their savings on daily living, healthcare, and other age-related expenses that in the past was largely unnecessary because the oldest son and his family often cared for his parents in the ancestral home. With more and more families living apart from one another, this dynamic has changed tremendously in the past decade or so.

I predict three things will occur in Japan in the future:

1) A sharp increase in taxes, especially sales tax. When I first came to Japan to live, there was no sales tax at all. The price on the product was the price you paid. The "bubble" debacle of the late 80s forced the government to implement a moderate sales tax initially, which was increased to 5%. This will most likely, at the very least, be doubled to 10%, perhaps more.

2) A raise in the amount of money people pay for socialized healthcare. The system here requires each worker to pay into the system and this amount is matched by the employer. I love the socialized healthcare system because I can show my card at any clinic or hospital in Japan and receive immediate treatment. The cost per visit is nominal, but this will most likely rise to offset the total cost of healthcare for the elderly. With the "top-heavy" configuration, there just are not enough young people paying into the system to keep it solvent. There must be an overhaul of the medical services that are now being dispensed in Japan. Japanese people have been conditioned to go to a doctor or a hospital at the drop of a hat for minor ailments like common colds and stomach aches.

Hospitals and doctors in Japan have a tendency to over prescribe medication and other expensive tests for relatively minor aches and pains. The current system makes it advantageous for them to do so because they receive money back from the government for every procedure performed. Currently, for any surgery or invasive treatment, patients usually stay in the hospital for one month. In countries that do not have a universal healthcare system, like the United States, private insurance companies want patients dismissed as soon as possible, sometimes on the same day as a surgery.

The system in place now in Japan must be reformed to make it more cost effective, efficient and solvent. Now that fewer and fewer elderly people are living with their children, placing the primary care of these people on the shoulders of the socialized healthcare system, excessive treatments must be stopped to save money for more serious ailments and diseases. Many elderly people go to the doctor or hospital on a daily basis as a sort of "social" gathering to see friends and to chat. These people arrive in the early morning to get a place in line and to see their friends, which plugs up the system for those who are truly in need of medical care that is more urgent. This is a burden on a system that is already strained.

3) A raise in the mandatory retirement age. Since retirees are living longer, often their quality of life is much better which allows them to work past the 60-65 retirement age. Luckily, many older people in Japan prefer to work and are quite happy to do so. With people living into their 90s, retiring at 60 means that many people have a three decade retirement.

The declining population in Japan has many colleges and universities wringing their hands. Attracting enough students to fill its slots is a challenge now, and will only get more competitive in the coming years as educational institutions of higher learning try to rethink their programs, doing what they can to stay afloat…my university included.

Finally, Japan will be forced to open its doors to more immigrants willing to relocate here to work. When this does happen, the face of Japan will change considerably. Within the next generation or so, Japan most likely will take on the appearance of a "mosaic" rather than the homogeneous face it now has. Actually, it is already happening.

[28] *Students in Japan Responsible for Cleaning their School...and Serving Lunch*

This might be surprising to students everywhere, but in Japan there are generally no janitors in schools to keep them clean. Each day, before the school day ends, the entire student body descends upon the school like a small army of ants to clean it from top to bottom. Every student is assigned a specific duty—sweeping the hallway, cleaning the toilets, emptying the trash cans—every conceivable chore that needs to be done to keep the school orderly, clean, and neat.

Japanese students cheerfully go about doing their assigned chores as it is just a part of their normal, daily school life. No one complains, at least outwardly, because everyone is expected to participate and to help out. The smaller kids are given tasks that they can do more easily, leaving the harder jobs to the older students.

When I first came to Japan 20 years ago, I taught English in a junior high school. I sometimes visited elementary schools as part of my teaching schedule. In those days, many schools did not have a formal cafeteria where students would eat their lunches. Each day, at about eleven o'clock in the morning, a truck would deliver big pots of food; each class had a rotating schedule of students who would go down to retrieve their class' food and dishes to bring back to the classroom.

The students would then arrange their desks into small groups and several other students would don white coats and hats to serve each student in an assembly line. The other students would line up with trays, chopsticks, and bowls to receive their lunch being served by their classmates. When everyone had their food, the class leader for the day would stand up and say *itadakimasu* (there is no good English translation for this phrase, but it's like saying "bon appétit"). This signaled that it was time to begin eating. When everyone had finished, the leader would stand and say *gochisosamadeshita*, a phrase which is said after a meal. It is sometimes translated as "thank you for the meal."

Each student then placed his/her tray, bowls, and chopsticks on a cart; the students who were assigned to work the lunch for that day gathered all of the pots and pans and wheeled all of it back down to the door where it was picked up by the food company. It all would be professionally washed and then prepared for the next day's lunch.

Lunch preparation by students in their homeroom class

Every week, each set of duties changed, allowing all of them to participate equally with the lunch service. This system saved the school from having to create an expensive cafeteria, taught students the importance of working as a group, and saved much cost from employing an on-site staff to prepare and clean-up after each lunch service.

Today, as schools have begun to modernize, they are beginning to adopt the idea of a big cafeteria, but many of the same duties and obligations involving the retrieval and serving of the food, as well as the after-lunch cleaning duties, are still performed by the students.

Perhaps by having students clean the school, and serve food to their peers at lunch, make Japanese students more appreciative of the effort it takes to keep a school clean and to serve lunch to an entire school every day. Certainly, Japanese students are much less likely to throw trash or garbage on the floor, or to damage property. After all, they will be the ones who will have to clean up the mess.

[29] *Japanese Educational System in Crisis—Recent Influx in Student Suicides Due to Bullying*

Few occurrences in life are more disturbing and sad than when a young person's life is cut short. It is indeed tragic if this occurs through illness, an accident, or by the hand of another. It is especially heart-rending when it is through suicide. Those who are left behind forever wonder if something could have been done to prevent what occurred.

In recent years, Japan has been rocked by a rash of student suicides. At the crux of this quandary is the sad fact that each of these cases is the result of bullying. In one particularly disturbing case, the student's teacher had encouraged the bullying by participating in it himself. As expected, the other students in the class intensified their bullying with the seeming approval of the teacher, interpreting his poor judgment as a sign of being able to do what and as they wished. The bullied student hung himself at the school. Ironically, in a bizarre twist, the student specified in his suicide note that any money left over after his funeral be given to his homeroom class—the very people who made his life so miserable that he felt he had no choice other than to kill himself. Even in death, he seemingly tried to seek their approval.

Collectively, as a society, there has been much hand wringing in Japan over the past few years, trying to come to some sort of conclusion as to why this is happening and with such frequency. Bullying or *ijime* has always been a problem in Japan, but one difference today is the constancy in which it is occurring, causing politicians and educators alike to speculate if it is indeed bordering on becoming a full-fledged epidemic.

There was a period when it seemed like a week hardly went by that the nightly news report did not begin with yet another suicide case by an elementary or junior high school-aged child; video footage of the telltale vase of flowers sitting on the lone desk in an empty classroom, marking the deceased student's seat. Of course, fingers are being pointed in every direction. Parents point to a breakdown in the school system where supervision of students is perhaps lax and a bullying mentality is either overlooked or even ignored; administrators point to the teachers, saying they should have been aware of the bullying which occurred under their noses; teachers pointing back at the parents and schools saying they cannot possibly stay on top of the situation with such a heavy workload, which includes the huge responsibility given to them as "homeroom" teachers who must oversee the "moral" education of the children in their care. The blame game comes full circle.

Rarely in Japan is one segment of society held accountable, taking responsibility categorically. Instead, blame is compartmentalized or divided somewhat equally over several components, making it difficult to discern or pinpoint exactly who is at fault or what exactly happened. As one well-known expert on Japan noted in his book, *The Enigma of Japanese Power*, Karl von Wolfren wryly concluded that the "buck" never really ever stops in Japan, but continues to get passed around until it does not really matter anymore.

For the sake of the children in extreme peril, I hope this will certainly not be the case in this instance. Alarmed by the sudden surge in preteen and teen suicide, former Prime Minister of Japan, Shinzo Abe, instructed a newly appointed council on education reform to make this a priority when he was in power, calling for sweeping and strict measures to be implemented against students who bully, and teachers who participate in bullying (or who fail to take appropriate action when a bullying situation is known). To outsiders, these criterions seem like no-brainers, but this shift in policy was quite unprecedented. A prevailing attitude in the past has been—perhaps unintentionally—to blame the victim by insisting the bullied students toughen up or try to adapt and fit into the standards set by the majority of the group. Former Prime Minister Abe broke with standard political protocol by sending a personal advisor on his behalf to southern Japan to meet with officials at the scene of one of the suicides. This act was unparalleled, considering that his predecessors in the past never bothered to intervene so directly.

The idea that day after day, a bullied student is forced to engage with those who are the tormentors is unfathomable. Is it any wonder, then, that the bullied children feel they have no other choice? In Japan, instead of teachers maintaining a classroom where students must move around the school to attend various classes with different classmates in each class, Japanese students are assigned to a "homeroom" class where the teachers come to the classroom to teach the lessons. All teachers have a desk in one big "teacher's room." So, for the most part, Japanese students are in the same classroom with the same classmates the entire time they are in school.

For a bullied student, this is a living nightmare. Between classes, students are largely unsupervised as the teachers all return to the teacher's room to prepare for the next lesson. Students congregate in the area around their classroom which means that bullied students are at the mercy of the bullies who have free reign during these breaks, at lunch, and before and after school. Perhaps changes will be made now that the bullying issue is central in the push to reform the educational system in Japan, cleaning house so to speak, rather than merely paying lip service to pacify voters. Only time will tell, and in the process, I hope that Japanese teachers have finally realized that ignoring bullying will not make it go away. Nipping it in the bud will.

Bullied students do not have many options in removing themselves from being terrorized by bullies. It is often difficult for bullied students to change schools in Japan, especially for elementary or junior high schools, because the custom is to attend the school nearest to the children's homes. Besides, if the child lives in a small town then there is likely no other choice but to attend the one public school. There are also documented cases where students simply refused to go to school, missing an entire academic year or more. This, for obvious reasons, is not a solution to the problem. "Home schooling" is virtually unheard of here in Japan, as well, with only a few families opting to home school. These families, ironically, are sometimes bullied by society for choosing not to follow a standard form of education for their children.

A new trend that has been reported recently are non-traditional schools that are specifically geared to the "square pegs" or students who have a difficult time fitting in socially to the more mainstream schools. These schools are few and far between, but in more cosmopolitan areas, they are gaining in popularity and are being more formally recognized as alternatives to the traditional public school system. One of the main problems with bullied students staying in their regular schools is that when they are bullied, they are also ostracized from the group, making them outcasts. For the bullied students to tell their parents or teachers would mean that they are bringing more attention to the fact that they do not fit into the "group."

This type of mental or emotional bullying is often as heinous, and in the long run more damaging, to the child as is physical abuse by the bullies. Also, by telling an adult puts the bullied child further at risk with the bullies if it is found out by the group that s/he told on them. Hence, often is the case where a bullied child suffers in silence hoping the situation will neutralize. Usually it does not and the situation is exacerbated—like sharks to blood in water, bullies prey upon the weak and disenfranchised. The group mentality that is rather pervasive in Japan further complicates the problem. Students tend to side with the majority. Once a child is singled out by the group, they often endure even more bullying from an even larger cross-section of the student population.

One particular example of this phenomenon, which saddened me greatly, occurred a number of years ago in Tokyo. It involved a student who was made a mockery by his classmates. During class, the students in the boy's class decided to mimic a funeral for him. They teased him incessantly about not being worthy to be alive. They forced him to lie on desks as if he were dead. The students all signed a "funeral card." More shocking, though, was that the teacher also signed the fake funeral card. All in fun? I think not; especially not to the poor boy who was humiliated and made to feel worthless by the bullying. He committed suicide shortly after this dreadful spectacle.

The current bullying issue in Japan has also involved, on occasion, schools and boards of education trying to cover-up suicide cases in order to save face. In fact, a number of suicides—which were initially deemed not to be the result of peer bullying—have been reversed and are now finally being regarded as being directly caused by bullying. Until this reversal, some school administrators tried to claim that there was insufficient evidence to prove bullying was a factor in a number of the suicides which occurred in their school systems. This is all the more unbelievable when considering that a number of the children had left detailed suicide notes naming the perpetrators.

I credit the tireless efforts of the grieving parents in these cases who diligently pushed forward, refusing to accept the conclusions of these schools that the children were not bullied. One father finally received vindication when school administrators visited his home to pay their respects at his child's Buddhist altar. They apologized for failing to recognize the child's death as a bullying-related suicide. The father was dignified in his response to them. He said that he hoped that if anything good could come from his ordeal, it would be to help prevent a similar occurrence from happening to another family.

Suicide due to bullying in Japan has been a simmering issue for many years. Parents feel helpless in protecting their children; schools have traditionally turned a blind eye to the problem. Now that it has exploded onto the front pages of newspapers, and is the lead story on nightly newscasts, something concrete hopefully will be done to put an end to bullying in schools. Let us hope for the sake of students still at risk that this attention will force those in power to implement political policy quickly to put an end—once and for all—to this malignancy that is chipping away at Japan's educational system, and ultimately, its soul.

Part V:

Cultural and Societal Miscellany

[30] *A Waving Cat Considered Good Luck in Japan*

I enjoy it when friends and family come to visit me in Japan. It gives me a chance to show them my Japanese life up-close and in-person. It also allows me the opportunity to see Japan through their eyes, as they experience Japanese daily life for the very first time. I call this the "fresh-eyes" approach because they often behold a part of Japanese culture that I no longer notice because it has become rather ordinary to me after living here for so many years. It is not until I return to the US for a visit that I think about how culturally different my everyday life really has become while living here.

A larger-than-life *manekineko* statue used to greet customers entering the restaurant

When I first arrived in Japan to live, I found everything to be exotic and fantastic. I certainly took a lot more photos in those days than I do now. I felt I had to get a photographic record of everything to prove that I was actually experiencing it.

Recently when two of my cousins came to visit, we took more pictures in the ten days they were here than I have taken in ten years. Everything fascinated them…and they wanted a digital record of it all. This was their first trip to Japan, so I made sure they got to see and experience a variety of different aspects of Japanese culture, life, traditions, and customs.

Immediately upon arriving, as we were going to our hotel in Tokyo, they noticed a custom which I am so used to now that I rarely ever take notice of it anymore: colorful ceramic cats with raised paws in shop windows…enticing passing customers to enter.

In many small shops, the owners place these cats either in the window or near the door as good luck charms. These cats have big eyes, are usually white with hand-painted accents around their faces and bodies, and always have one paw raised in a beckoning fashion. These cats are called *manekineko* and the idea behind the raised paw is to beckon customers into the shop, which in turn brings in cash. If the *manekineko* is waving its left paw, this is to bring in more customers; if the feline is raising its right paw, it is to bring in more money. White cats are considered to be lucky, black cats are used to protect the premises against evil spirits, and red cats are used to ward off bad luck and evil.

Besides the traditional uses of these friendly felines, fashion conscious young people are choosing *manekineko* that have a variety of shapes, sizes, colors, and textures that are more trendy. This proves that not only shop owners are benefiting from having the waving cats around—individuals are displaying them in their homes and offices, as well, to help make these spaces luckier in matters of not only money... but even love.

How did this tradition begin? It is difficult to know the true origin, but one popular legend that I heard from an elderly Japanese friend tells of a feudal lord who was caught in a deluge. As he was making his way down the street, he noticed a cat at a temple motioning to him with its paw to come in out of the rain. He obeyed the cat's request and was so grateful to the cat that he became a regular worshiper at the temple. His presence at the temple encouraged others to start attending, which in turn made the temple very rich.

Another version of how this legend got started featured a *geisha* courtesan who was narrowly saved from being bitten by a poisonous snake. Her feline companion suddenly raised its paw and waved it toward the snake, successfully fending off the snake attack. This protective gesture by her cat surely saved her from being bitten. Hence, having a waving cat near you was considered to be very fortuitous. No matter what the true origin of this custom is, the tradition of having a beckoning cat in stores or homes is here to stay. Some of the cats are quite elaborate, but most are smallish in size with modest decoration adorning its head and body.

Cat lovers will be pleased to know that there is a movement afoot in Japan to make September 29th the national *manekineko* day because the date 9/29 can be pronounced *kuru fuku* in Japanese which means "may luck come." Japanese will often connect words to the pronunciation of numbers. For instance, I remember when a large department store chain in Japan had a 39 yen sale after its baseball team won its division. The sound of the numbers 3 and 9 are *san kyu* which in English sounds like "thank you." It was the store's way of saying "thank you" to its customers.

I do suggest, however, that if you ever encounter a live waving cat that you pay special attention to your surroundings, especially if it is not raining. After all, it could be warning you of a snake that is too close for comfort…or it could just be a friendly cat. If you are in front of a store, take note of which paw it is using—a raised left paw wants you as a customer, and a waving right paw wants your cash. Either way, the cat gets you where it counts—in the wallet.

[31] *Japanese Phrases Associated with Cats*

When I was first learning Japanese, I noticed a similarity between English and Japanese in that there are a lot of phrases that refer to "cats." The first such phrase I remember learning in Japanese literally translates to "cat's tongue." It is used when someone takes a bite of hot food and says *nekojita*, meaning "the food is too hot for my tongue." Of course, a similar phrase in English that people often use is "does the cat have your tongue?" These two sayings have completely different meanings, but the reference each one makes to "cats" and "tongues" is what interested me.

The term "cat burglar" refers to the stealthy movement a robber makes in the shadows, skulking about, similar to that of a cat. The Japanese phrase, *nekobaba*, is the slang term used for crooked politicians or government officials who pocket public funds. It can also be used like the English phrase "finders keepers, losers weepers;" meaning that something found on a road or somewhere is a form of *nekobaba*. I found each Japanese person I would ask about this phrase would have a different idea about its meaning. I have personally heard it used with someone who has a tendency to pilfer little things from a public place—like a salt shaker from a table in a restaurant. Interestingly, though, both phrases disparage cats by relating them to an act of "thieving."

Nekome is a phrase I occasionally heard early on in my tenure in Japan but I had a hard time figuring out the exact meaning of this expression. Literally it means "cat's eye," but in practice conveys "good eyesight," so I immediately thought of the old-style "cat eye" glasses that were so popular in the 1950s. This had nothing to do with the true meaning of the phrase, however. *Nekome* is, in fact, very closely related to a common English phrase that means the same thing. It refers to the way cats' eyes shine in the light at night (e.g., "He was so shocked at the news that he stood there "like a cat in headlights").

The Japanese phrase—*nekoze*—does not really have a good English equivalent, but is easily visualized and understood when the connection is made: This phrase refers to a cat's arched back, and is used in reference to people who are slump-shouldered or who are slightly hunch-backed.

Stray cats looking for handouts at a Tokyo apartment building

A number of Japanese cat-related phrases make logical sense when explained clearly. For instance, the term *neko nade goe* means "cat's voice" but more accurately means to lure someone to you with a coaxing voice, like a kitten meowing to get some milk.

Neko ka buri is "camouflage" but would probably be translated into English as "a wolf in sheep's clothing." The English phrases "everybody and his brother" or "every Tom, Dick and Harry" are similar to the

Japanese saying *neko mo shakushi mo*. It literally means "even cats and ladles," meaning "everybody."

Geisha were once referred to as *neko* because the stringed instrument they were trained to play—the *shamisen*—was traditionally made from cat skin. I imagine the name also has something to do with the mystery surrounding *geisha*, and their enigmatic behavior that could be defined as "cat-like."

Cats originally came to Japan via Korea and China in ancient times. Until around the 10th century, they were quite rare and esteemed. In the 12th century, it appears that cats became more commonplace and everyday people began to have them as pets. Initially, long-tailed cats were preferred but during the Edo period (1600-1868), stubby-tailed cats gained in popularity. I sometimes see these short-tailed cats and they look so unnatural with their stubby little tails. After all, cats often express themselves with their tails; their graceful movements as they move their perfectly erect tails resemble the tall plants with the fuzzy spikes we call "cattails."

The Japanese word for "pussy willow" is *neko ya nagi* which clearly contains the "cat" reference. In English, we take a "cat nap," a person who is fearful of even simple things is a "scaredy cat," and a brawl between two women is often called a "cat fight." In both languages, there are a number of cat references—some similar in meaning, others not.

Although I would not consider myself a "cat" person, I do like cats and find them intriguing. Several years ago when I entered my backyard here in Japan, I was startled by a huge "tomcat" sunning himself on my deck. He looked at me, I looked at him. There was a seemingly mutual understanding between us as we sized each other up. I guess he intuitively knew that he was welcome to use my deck whenever he wanted.

With a flick of his big tail, the deal was sealed as he lazily shut his eyes and continued his nap, enjoying the comfort and security of my porch every afternoon for the remainder of the summer.

[32] *Every Dog has Its Day...Especially the Pampered Ones in Japan*

When I first came to Japan to live, I remember being amazed at the lack of stray dogs wandering the streets. I did see the occasional stray cat, but rarely did I ever see a dog—and when I did, I am sure it had gotten loose from its owner accidentally and was not a stray. In those days, a goodly number of Japanese people did keep dogs, but almost exclusively as "outside" pets, which meant they were tied on a short rope or chain to a tiny doghouse or other makeshift cover…and sometimes with no protection at all from the elements. There was no chance for the dog to escape, run, play, or do "dog" things, like exploring, digging, tracking, and of course, sniffing anything and everything. This distressed me to see these pets relegated to a life of being tied up and left outside in all sorts of weather. Since most homes have no real yard to speak of, dogs were often kept in narrow passageways next to the house.

A pampered "inside" Japanese pet suns itself on the living room furniture

Previously, people did not really walk their dogs nor have any real, meaningful interaction with them. The apartment I lived in when I first relocated to Japan was in a residential area. A neighbor had one of these "tied-up" dogs; the poor thing howled night and day from boredom and depression. Pets back then, especially dogs, were basically regarded as possessions and not considered to be an extension of the family unit.

An American friend I know visited a family back in the early 90's and commented that the family dog seemed cold as it slept on the snow outside the front stoop. The owner replied that the dog "liked" sleeping on the snow-covered ground. The owner's child, however, piped up and said that she remembered one winter when they let the dog inside the house and it seemed to like sleeping inside the warm, cozy home as well. Uh-huh. I am sure if given a real choice, we can guess which place the dog would choose to sleep. Fast forward a couple of decades and I am happy to report that the situation has changed completely, with pet dogs being indulged by pet owners in an unprecedented manner. The "pet boom" of the past few years in Japan has turned owners here into doting masters that resemble that of European and North American countries where pet ownership is taken very seriously.

Traditionally, many homes in Japan used *tatami* (straw mats) as floor coverings which were quite fragile and very high-maintenance. It was virtually unthinkable to allow pets inside where they could soil, scratch, claw, and potentially destroy these very expensive and delicate coverings. Today, many new homes tend to use more durable coverings like hardwood floors and linoleum. This has made it more practical to have "inside" pets that do become like family members. I recently read a very interesting statistic which also might explain the recent surge in pet ownership in Japan, which has encouraged masters to embrace their pets completely, treating them like small children. Japanese families now own over 23 million pet dogs and cats, a figure which now exceeds the number of Japanese children who are under the age of 15. In 2006, the number of children under the age of 15 was under 18 million.

Since Japan has been suffering from a yearly decrease in population for several years, I think that childless couples and singles here are substituting the love and care they would normally give to a child to their pets. Animal companions are not only trendy, but fulfill an apparent emotional need for people who want to have some type of physical interaction with another living thing. Caring for a pet allows them to love the pet unconditionally, while receiving the same in return. A case in point: A good friend stopped by my home with his wife; when he exited the car I noticed he was sitting in the backseat. When I asked why he was being chauffeured he said, "Oh, Pochi gets the front seat, so I have to sit in the back." They have no children, so their poodle is a surrogate child, of sorts, because his wife fawns over this dog as if it were a child. Later that same day, we drove to a coffee shop that has an outside patio that allows pet owners the opportunity to bring their pets with them. Of course, my friend and I sat in the backseat, while Pochi sat shotgun in the front with his wife.

My friend's wife had a backpack filled with treats, water, a portable dish, food, toys, and a little coat for Pochi. She prepared all of these things in anticipation of any need the little dog might have while on this little outing. Perhaps she represents the modern or stereotypical pet owner in Japan. The majority of animal owners currently spend a lot of time and money on their pets, making the pet industry in Japan a very lucrative and ever-expanding business. It was reported that nearly nine billion US dollars was spent in one year by Japanese animal lovers on pet-related items. Although it is a fourth of what Americans spend on pets every year, it represents nearly a 50% increase since the mid-1990s when pets were basically left outside and ignored.

A family dog even gets in the Christmas mood by donning a doggie Santa suit, hoping for a bite from the table

Another group of people who have embraced pet ownership in Japan are older or retired people. Couples who have grown children that live away, find having animal companions to be good company, giving them a purpose which fills the need to care and love another living thing. Also, since young couples are having fewer children, this means that older couples do not have as many grandchildren. In addition, in the past, the oldest child usually would live with the parents, giving them companionship and a purpose. Today, more and more elderly couples are finding that their children are living separately, leaving them to live on their own. Owning a pet fills an emotional void that some older couples have—to feel needed or useful, while also allowing them to channel their energies of love and caring toward another living thing.

Indulgent pet owners can go overboard, trying to feed their pets food that is best reserved for human consumption. This has led to diseases like obesity, diabetes and heart ailments. A Japanese friend loved to give her little trio of Dachshunds bites from the table; they especially were fond of cheese. Suddenly, one day the little one was lethargic and unusually low-key. A quick trip to the veterinarian revealed that the dog's penchant for cheese did not agree with its system. With the aid of a laxative, the dog was all right in the end, but the doctor scolded my friend and suggested she put all her pets on a strict diet. She spoiled them out of love, but realized it was not in their best interest to do so.

In general, Japanese people are influenced greatly by trends and fads which affect their decision-making when purchasing items related to clothing, cars, and even pets. When the movie *101 Dalmatians* first hit the silver screen, a number of people rushed out to buy one of these dogs. The problem was that as puppies they were cute and cuddly, but soon grew to be very large dogs, requiring a lot of space and care. Apartment living is best suited for smaller canines, and not the larger ones. Also, Dalmatians are not necessarily known for their sweetness toward small children, having a tendency to be nippy if provoked. The end result was that many of these impulsive owners were forced to unload these dogs because of the impracticality of keeping them in a small space with small children.

Another example, which is still currently a trend, is Chihuahuas. A number of years ago, a loan commercial aired on TV featuring a long-haired Chihuahua; instantly there was a Chihuahua boom. Pet shops could not keep up with the great demand for these animals, so this caused the price of these dogs to skyrocket. The loan company, after seeing the huge potential of this sudden fad, decided to make this Chihuahua a part of its ongoing advertising campaign. Cleverly, the company continued riding the boom it created by using this dog in a number of different scenarios, one of which featured it married with little Chihuahua puppies all around. People could not get enough of this cute little Chihuahua and had to have one. This is not too much unlike the US boom that occurred after the airing of the talking Chihuahua dog in the Taco Bell commercials. Similarly, Taco Bell used this interest to market a variety of goods featuring that big-eyed, adorable dog, creating a whole industry around this one character.

Many Japanese pet owners relish owning a unique or unusual type of dog with rare features, making it highly prized. For instance, if the animal has an alternative coat color to what is the norm, or has two different eye colors, or is so small it can fit into a handbag, people clamor to buy these from pet stores. This is the problem. The demand is outstripping the supply, tempting breeders to produce more dogs more quickly. Unscrupulous dog breeders, trying to make as much money as they can, are breeding parent dogs with offspring, siblings, etc in order to keep up with the high demand. The sad result is that more and more dogs are being born with severe genetic disorders, causing pain and suffering to the dogs, and heartbreak to the doting owners.

Some of the genetic diseases are obvious from the time the dogs are born, but others stay hidden until years later when the symptoms suddenly appear, causing the owner to endure an emotional rollercoaster, not to mention spending huge amounts of money, trying to cure or care for the animal. The newly reformed Japanese pet owner will spend any amount of money, like devoted pet owners everywhere, to save a pet which is like a child or family member.

Very good friends of mine recently learned this lesson the hard way. Their little boy so desperately wanted a pet dog. They agreed that a toy poodle which is small and does not shed hair would be the best choice. They purchased the dog from a breeder. The dog was perfectly fine for several months, and then one day it had a seizure and died on the way to the veterinarian's office. Although an autopsy was inconclusive as to the exact cause, it is well-known that one symptom of over-breeding are brittle bones. The dog's skull was fractured and the brain hemorrhaged. Needless to say, the little boy was crushed.

He grieved by making a Buddhist altar for his little dog, arranging her photo and toys around the cremated remains. The entire family was completely heartbroken.

Japanese pet owners sometimes pay anywhere from $8,000-$10,000 dollars for some of these rare or highly sought after dogs with unusual features. What is not clearly understood by these people is that in order to get a Dachshund with white fur (very rare) or a Chihuahua with a bluish coat, the dog, which has a recessive gene, is bred over and over with direct offspring who also will likely have the same recessive gene in order to get that peculiarity. One puppy with the desired characteristic in a litter may be healthy while all the others are grossly deformed or crippled—no eyes, one paw missing, mentally deficient. But, unethical breeders still feel that selling one for $10,000 is worth the effort, regardless if the majority of the litter has to be put down.

This problem unfortunately is not unique to Japan. Similar cases abound in the United States as well. One difference, however, is the amount of regulations in place to protect animals and pet owners in America from unethical breeders. This, in time, will also be the norm in Japan because the pet boom shows no signs of declining anytime soon, and pet owners will demand changes be made to protect not only them, but the animals at risk.

I currently do not own a pet because of my hectic work and travel schedule. It just would not be fair to the animal. But, if and when I do get a pet, it will likely be a dog and it will be one that comes to me through rescue or adoption. Some of the best dogs I have ever known are the ones who are just run-of-the-mill dogs, so mixed that it is impossible to discern clearly which breed is dominant. They are often hearty, healthy, loving and, if rescued or adopted, very appreciative companions.

[33] *There's Something Fishy Going on in Japan*

Having lived in Japan for so long, I have become quite acculturated to the Japanese way, including customs, traditions, and daily life. There is one particular area, though, that I have never developed a taste for and that is some types of Japanese food, especially fish.

Unfortunately, I am not a fish-eater, which makes living on an island problematic at best. Many Japanese dishes use some type of piscine or piscatorial flavoring, including fish stock, making it quite difficult at times to find something that is totally fish-free.

Believe me, I have tried to eat just about everything at least once over the years and if I were to be blindfolded and given a taste test, I swear I would be able to identify the foods that have the minutest amount of fish flavor in them.

Friends will always urge me to taste things I know I will clearly not like. "Oh, this has no fishy taste at all, trust me. Just try it." Nanoseconds later I am disposing of it in a napkin—similar to the way a baby who tastes something it does not like, letting the foul tasting foreign object roll right out of its mouth and onto the floor. I have stopped humoring people for the sake of politeness. After more than 20 years of testing this theory, I figure I am rather certain that seafood, or the slightest hint of fish, is not for me.

When I first arrived in Japan to live, I remember spying a bag of breaded onion rings in the freezer section at my favorite grocery store. I was so overjoyed that I grabbed the bag up and purchased these wonderful little things. Once home, I could hardly wait to bake them in order to savor that glorious taste of my childhood. However, as the succulent looking onion rings began to bake, an odd aroma filled the air. The more they baked, the stronger the odor became. I hurriedly opened the oven, pulled out the tray to cut one open to see from what these "onion" rings were made, and horror of horrors...they were not onion rings at all. I was cooking breaded "squid" rings.

Needless to say, the entire package was promptly put into the garbage and taken outside. A lot of air-freshener was used to cover the smell of baking squid which permeated every inch of my apartment. I learned a very valuable lesson with that experience: when something looks too good to be true, it probably is. I was much more careful in the future when purchasing a product solely based on pictures to show what is contained in the package.

I was a slow learner in those early years, I suppose, because I also remember buying a bag of chips that looked to be covered with some type of herb, like basil or sage. To my chagrin, the chips were sprinkled with flakes of seaweed. Most people who have only a slight aversion to seafood would most likely eat them without noticing. Not me. One bite and I knew it was from the sea. No thank you.

Shelled whelks for sale at a Japanese fish market[5]

Often people will order something in a restaurant to share with the table, like pasta, that has clams, tuna, or some other type of seafood cooked in the sauce. It amuses me when they recommend I just pick out the big pieces and eat the rest as if it had not been there from the beginning.

It is akin, in my opinion, to having a smoking section in a restaurant. The idea that the cigarette smoke will stay in one place and not spread is (in the words of a dear Hoosier friend) like having a "peeing section in a swimming pool"—no matter whether it is smoke, urine, or fish sauce—it makes no difference. Once it is out in the general area, there is no corralling it back.

People sometimes try to fool me...which is next to impossible. "Oh, there's no fish in this, promise!" One bite makes me beg to differ, which then prompts the person to say, "Oh, you don't eat tuna either?" [Any myriad of seafood or fish can be substituted for the tuna example: shrimp, oysters, clams, lobster, and caviar, *ad infinitum*.] I really think they are just playing dumb in these cases, because it is astounding that intelligent people think that something from the ocean, which lives in water, is not fish.

"Uh, yeah, if it comes from an ocean, river, lake, or creek and swims or lives in the water, I would categorize that as 'fish,' thank you very much." People who know me well, do not even try to slip me a dish laced with some sort of fish, no matter how small the amount, because they know that I will detect it. That is a statistical certainty.

Perhaps because I grew up in landlocked Indiana (unless you count Lake Michigan in the northern part of the state), or the fact that as a child my family never ate fresh fish, are reasons why I just never developed a taste for it. I figure at my age, I probably will not be developing this taste anytime soon, seeing I live in a place that is renowned for its fresh fish and gorgeous seafood.

As I mentioned before, over the years I have tried everything of the fishy variety and there is not anything I remotely like. Grilled eel and sea cucumber (trust me it is not a vegetable) were the most unpleasant things I have ever tasted. Of course, there are people who gobble these delicacies down licking their lips for more, but not me. Maybe it was the texture I could not get past. Eel is very stringy, in my opinion, and sea cucumber was just too chewy. It seemed the more I chewed, the more it multiplied in my mouth. The most unpleasant 30 seconds of my life, bar nothing else.

Sushi lovers, I am sure, are bereft at the thought that I could eat *sushi* everyday of the week if I wanted but choose not to do so. Aomori, where I live in Japan, is well known for *hotate*—scallops. People come from all over Japan to sample these shelled creatures, sending boxes to friends and family via special refrigerated trucks. People eat them by the dozens. When strangers ask where I live and I mention Aomori, automatically two things come to their minds—scallops and apples. I always gear the conversation toward the apples.

To demonstrate how much of a purist I am, once when I was served a cold mug of beer I took one sip and had to set it down. The mug it came in was molded from squid, which after the beer is drank can be eaten like beef jerky. A waste of a good mug of beer, in my opinion, not to mention the "squid mug" it came in.

To counteract any do-gooders who undoubtedly tried to convert me into a fish-eater during my current stint of living in Japan, I confidently informed everyone early on that I was terribly allergic to seafood and fish. This worked like a charm. No one ever tried to force fish on me again. Some people even went as far as sniffing out the slightest hint of seafood, becoming a sort of "fish" detective on my behalf, ensuring that I not get hold of anything that had the least bit of fish in it.

Once this is published, I suppose my cover will be blown. I am not worried about anyone trying to get me to eat any fish product because

I still have a few tricks up my sleeve to avoid fish-related situations. These, however, will remain a secret to keep people on their guard.

[34] *Harvest Time in Japan*

Autumn in Japan signals not only the end of summer, but harvest time. The telltale sign that fall has arrived in Japan is the hustle-bustle of the farmers who work feverishly from sunup to sundown to bring in their crops. Of course, instead of fields of corn as far as the eye can see, rice paddies dot Japan's landscape from north to south.

Whenever I call a dear friend in rural Indiana, her husband—true to his farming roots—always wants to know: What's the weather like over there? American farmers are obsessed with the weather, and Japanese farmers are no different. They too have to try to guess when is the best time to bring in the crops in order not to risk lowering their yield; or worse, losing product due to an early frost. Growing rice is especially tricky because the conditions must be just right for it to grow to maturation.

Rice hanging to dry on poles in a recently harvested rice field

When I first relocated to Japan, there was an unseasonably cool summer one year which caused severe damage to the rice plants. For germination to occur, rice grows best in climates that are humid with high temperatures. However, that particular year was an agricultural nightmare because of the cool summer weather that plagued the entire archipelago. Very little rice was harvested, leaving Japan in a very precarious situation. How would Japan be able to supply its people with the favored *Japonica* variety of short, sticky rice?

The only option, and one that Japan tried to avoid but ultimately could not, was to import rice from other countries like Australia, Thailand and the United States. It was a sobering moment for the farmers and Japanese people in general. Japanese people tend to prefer homegrown rice to imported rice because it is believed the quality of Japanese rice is superior to other countries' products. Also, the texture is glutinous which makes it "sticky," a feature that Japanese people insist upon.

It would be akin to Midwesterners in the United States being forced to import "sweet-corn" from South America; even though it may be just as good as the corn in Iowa, Illinois or Indiana, there is a certain degree of snobbery involved, and the average Midwesterner would much rather have fresh, home-grown corn as opposed to an imported facsimile.

Since rice (*kome* in Japanese) is the principal crop of Japan, and is believed to have been introduced initially by either China or Korea during the Yayoi Period (circa 300 BC – 300 AD), the history of rice production extends to the very core of the Japanese-self. The entire Japanese extended family system is believed to have evolved around the rice culture: planting, cultivating, and harvesting. Traditionally, rice farming required an inordinate amount of communal cooperation between families and neighbors due to the great care it takes to grow the rice, which includes a very sophisticated system of water irrigation that often times must pass through a neighbor's paddy to reach one's own paddy.

Through this type of communal cooperation, the agricultural system developed thousands of years ago which has helped to mold Japanese society and culture into what it is today. This, in part, is why Japanese people work very hard to maintain harmony (*wa*) between neighbors and colleagues in order to avoid strife and conflict. As a people, or society, Japanese have learned how best to live within a tight-knit community through this type of cooperation. With such a long agricultural history, as expected, the planting and cultivation of rice gradually took on religious implications over the millennia and many festivals occur each spring and autumn to honor *Shinto* deities connected to this all important staple food.

Many years ago, I was invited by an American friend who married a Japanese farmer to experience harvesting rice. It was quite an operation (from start to finish) which makes me much more mindful of the process and work involved each time I pick up chopsticks to shovel rice into my mouth.

My particular job was to go along and gather the bundles of cut rice; these then had to be balanced on poles (using only a small stick tied with twine at the base) so it could dry. There was certainly a skill to doing it properly because on more than one occasion the entire stack tumbled to the ground, forcing me to start the process all over again. My friend's father-in-law was quite entertained throughout the day by my antics. Even though I hail from Indiana, my time spent in a farming environment is severely limited.

After the rice dries and is removed from the fields, the stubble that is left on the ground is then burned. Every year, when the wind blows in a certain direction, the streets of my city are blanketed in a smoky haze which permeates every nook and cranny. I asked a farmer-friend here why Japanese farmers burn the fields every year and he explained to me that coupled with fertilization, this is the best way to maintain the ground so that it can be cultivated year after year without any ill effects to the soil. Somehow the scorching effect has a positive influence on the soil.

Besides rice, the area where I live is well-known for its delectable apples. Apples were first introduced to Japan in the early Meiji Period (1868-1912). The prefecture where I live, Aomori, is by far the largest and most famous apple-producing area in all of Japan. Along with rice fields, apple orchards are sprinkled throughout the countryside and on the cities' edges.

The first apple seeds to find their way to this area were brought by a missionary teacher named John Ing. He was affiliated with the same Methodist group that started the university where I teach. Coincidentally, Mr. Ing (like myself) came from central Indiana. He was affiliated with Asbury University in Greencastle, now called DePauw University. Mr. Ing is known in these parts as the "Johnny Appleseed of Japan" because of his contribution to the apple industry. Little did he know then what a huge impact his little gift would have upon the agricultural and economic stability of this region some 120 years later.

Although I technically live in the city, within a five-minute bicycle ride from my home, I am deep in apple country with orchards lining both sides of the road. Please remember, when I say "orchards" I am not talking about a 500 acre spread of perfectly lined trees with wide avenues between them; instead, Japanese orchards tend to be very compact, with the trees so close together that a small vehicle is sometimes unable to drive between them.

A typical apple orchard with some apples still covered and others reddening before being picked

In early spring, once the buds have come and gone, each apple is hand-wrapped with a paper bag to insure that it is not weather damaged or preyed upon by insects. Pesticides are also used to fight pestilential predators. Apple farmers regularly attend to the trees throughout the summer until harvest time. Once it is nearing the time for harvest, the bags used to wrap the apples are individually removed from each one and large metallic sheets are gingerly placed under the trees to reflect the sun. The reflective sheets help to insure that the color of each apple is uniform. No one would want an apple that is red on top and a different color on the bottom!

Apple farming is somewhat of a cottage industry in this area, with many rice farmers dabbling with apples in addition to cultivating their rice crop. Many small orchards are basically in the backyards of farmers' homes, utilizing every available inch of space for their crops. Of course, there are bigger operations that have a significant number of trees within a particular orchard, but the majority tends to be smaller "Mom & Pop" affairs that depend upon the nuclear and extended family to do the bulk of the work.

Every spring a goodly portion of my students return home on the weekends to assist their families with rice planting, and then in the fall, the same students return home to assist with the harvest and to help pick the apples for market. Each year, students bring me bags upon bags of wonderful apples from their farms which I appreciate greatly. People in Tokyo and beyond have to pay dearly for the same apples I enjoy on a daily basis.

Picking the apples especially takes a lot of time. Unlike rice harvesting, which is mostly mechanized today, apple farming utilizes a distinctly human touch. In fact, nearly all of the work in the apple industry here is done by hand, and even if the farmers wanted to use heavy machinery to cultivate the apples, it would be next to impossible to get the machines into the orchards. The apple trees are pruned to remain small in circumference and short in height, so ordinary step ladders can be used to attend to the branches, buds, and eventually to pick the apples.

As expected, the trees are planted very close together in order to save valuable space. There is seemingly no rhyme or reason to how they are planted, meaning there are no straight rows of trees usually. They are planted in the available space, in any way they can, utilizing every bit of accessible land. Also, there is a small window of opportunity after the apples have ripened at the end of October and early November to get the apples picked before it begins to snow.

Once I had an opportunity to help pick apples. It is back-breaking work because each apple must be removed carefully as not to bruise or mar it in anyway. The idea is to keep the apples as perfect as possible, in order to fetch the highest price possible. Apples are graded and selected, with the lowest quality apples used as juice and the highest quality ones being sold individually in gift sets.

A commercial company will sometimes hire an apple farmer to maintain specific trees for its clients. During the ripening stage, a stencil is put on the apple and as it ripens the company's logo becomes visible. These make for a unique calling card when an employee meets a customer.

The *kanji* character on these apples is *kotobuki*, which means "congratulations"

Also, a person's image can even be emblazoned on an apple by the use of a stencil. As a special gift, a person can be given an apple with their likeness and name on the skin of the fruit. Other popular slogans on apples feature the Japanese characters for "good luck" or "congratulations." These are given as gifts to students who are trying to pass the entrance exam into university or to a couple who are about to be married.

There is one sinister side to apple farming that makes farmers hold their breath every year around autumn—typhoons. A typhoon can literally decimate an entire season's crop in one day if the winds knock the apples to the ground, making them unsuitable for human consumption.

During my second year in Japan, a catastrophic typhoon hit this area and my city, Hirosaki, was at ground zero. The damage was tremendous with millions of apples littering the ground around the trees. As many as possible were made into juice, but the amount was so overwhelming that the companies that produced the juice could not keep up with the demand; the result— apples were left rotting on the ground.

Eventually, they were gathered and buried, but the devastation was too much for some farmers. The psychological toll was too great prompting a number of farmers to commit suicide, knowing that they would not be able to recover from the great economic loss. Perhaps insurance money was the only way they could hope to recover, leaving their families to pick up the pieces.

[35] *Neighborhood Associations in Japan*

Communities all over Japan have a unique system of "neighborhood associations," known as *chonaikai* in Japanese. These quasi-governmental organizations are responsible for assisting in local administrative functions, distributing important information, coordinating social activities, and planning neighborhood festivals.

The history of *chonaikai* dates back to the Edo Period (1600-1868); the current system is directly descended from the original prototype which was initially formed to hold local residents communally responsible for maintaining law and order in their neighborhoods, preserving moral propriety, and even to collect taxes. Once the Meiji Restoration (1868) started, and a push to modernize Japan began (this was the subject featured in Tom Cruise's film *The Last Samurai*), these local associations lost favor with governmental officials, and eventually forfeited the legal authority they once enjoyed.

A neighborhood bulletin board announcing events and displaying public service messages

However, in the 1920s, the system gradually reappeared in neighborhoods in the urban centers and slowly spread over the country. In 1940, the militarists who were running Japan saw a very lucrative and efficient way to maintain order and made *chonaikai* mandatory in all cities across the country. At this time, the neighborhood associations were given a variety of responsibilities which expanded their authority including the distribution of government rations, training residents in the civil defense of the community, and even being in charge of silencing any protests against the government.

After World War II, the US Occupation Forces abolished the system because it was viewed as being too authoritarian and even anti-democratic. Gradually, however, the 1950s reintroduced a pared down system of community organizations, making these neighborhood associations largely volunteer bodies that assisted the local governments in the distribution of materials including community announcements, city-related information (like various governmental reports) and local notices regarding neighborhood festivals and social activities.

Today, just as it was in the 1950s, these associations maintain a significant role in the social lifeline for communities all across Japan. The system allows for regular contact between neighbors and neighborhoods, giving them a social purpose. In my case, I look forward to receiving the telltale clipboard (*kairanban*) propped up against my door, placed there by the neighbor to the right of my home.

Once I have perused all of the announcements and notices, I walk it over to my neighbor on the other side. After they read through all of the information, they take it to the next neighbor until everyone has had a chance to see it. Often is the case where neighbors will stand and chat for a bit when exchanging the *kairanban*.

This system saves quite a bit of money. Since announcements (and the paper they come on) are shared, there is no need for mass-producing reams of notices. Also, this system reduces the cost of having to pay someone to walk them door-to-door, or potentially more costly, mailing them to each individual household. The local government makes great use of this system, saving it manpower and money.

Each household in the association takes a turn being in charge of collecting the yearly dues, passing out the newsletter, and overseeing the general running of the association for that particular street. Each of these leaders from the local associations reports to a general leader who oversees a larger area that encompasses a number of the smaller associations. This person then meets with the other larger associations and the local government.

A few years ago, the general association in the expanded area to where my neighborhood group is attached, built a beautiful new community center that can be reserved by residents living in one of the connected associations. Often, elderly people will use the facility for informal luncheons (it has a kitchen), making handicrafts, and to have social gatherings and get-togethers. Of course, the various neighborhood associations hold meetings there as well.

In addition to the clipboard that is passed from house to house, large community bulletin boards are placed in prominent places throughout the neighborhoods that post pertinent information for passersby to read. These include local notices, governmental campaigns, and general information that residents may need to know regarding upcoming events and festivals.

One function that the local neighborhood associations have been involved with is overseeing the proper recycling of household garbage. Every so often, as I stumble at the crack of dawn to the designated place where garbage is picked up, I am greeted by a person wearing an officious looking armband who is there to make sure that residents are not improperly disposing of garbage on the wrong day. I am unsure whether these people have any real authority, but they certainly can "shame" a person into compliance quite quickly. A scolding will ensue if one is trying to slip unauthorized garbage onto the pile on a day that it is not scheduled to be picked up. Something I would never attempt!

[36] *Recycling Garbage Serious Business in Japan*

When friends and family come to visit me here in Japan, I have to watch them like a hawk when it comes to the disposing of unwanted items in the wastebasket. My city, Hirosaki, has one of the most stringent recycling programs in the country. People from home are so used to tossing everything into one container that it is hard for them to break the habit of disposing unwanted items directly into the wastebasket without thought. Admittedly, I have to even pay special attention to Japanese friends visiting from other areas because they have a difficult time in knowing "what trash goes where." They are often surprised at how strict my city's recycling regulations are in comparison to where they live.

Recently, however, my city has relaxed the rules a bit due to the high cost to recycle plastics, allowing its citizenry to now place most plastic items in the "burnable" bin. This is unfortunate on many levels, not least of which is the environment. The entire city had been conditioned to separate all plastics for a number of years, and now is allowed to dump it all together—mind boggling.

Generally, all over Japan, people are required to sort their garbage into four basic categories: burnable, plastics, metals, and glass. My city has taken this one step further by subdividing these into even more groupings, within the main categories. We are expected to divide our garbage into twelve different categories, which is quite a problem for people who live in a one or two room apartment.

When this system first went into effect, the city distributed videos among all of the neighborhood associations (*chonaikai*). Neighborhoods in Japan are grouped together into small alliances; residents living in a particular area form an association and pay a nominal monthly stipend to be a part of this organization. In return, each household receives weekly announcements on a clipboard that is passed from neighbor to neighbor with bulletins about upcoming festivals, city ordinances, etc. Once the resident sees the information on the clipboard, it is passed to the next neighbor.

A designated trash heap on the morning it is picked up; netting is used to keep crows from scavenging

One month, instead of the usual papers being circulated around the neighborhood, a video was included to be watched by everyone in each household. The video was semi-professionally made, featuring a middle-aged housewife cheerfully separating her garbage into various containers while consulting a prescribed poster that outlines exactly how it is to be done. She even went as far as to wash out cans, bottles and the plastic food pouches found in instant-types of meals. She had rigged a small clothesline above her sink that she used to dry the plastic bags before disposing of them into the proper receptacle.

Most people I know could not be bothered with such detail, but the vast majority of people here separates their garbage and is quite dedicated to doing it properly. I certainly do not fudge on the prescribed manner of separating garbage for fear of being caught by a nosey neighbor or by one of the roving patrols of volunteer "garbage police" who occasionally make surprise visits at the collection points to make sure people are not improperly disposing their trash on the wrong day.

My city issued (in Japanese and English) a detailed poster to assist residents in the correct way to sort their trash. Towards the bottom of this poster, the phrase "Let's reduce our garbage" screams out to the reader to make it seem fun; next to it, however, is an ominous warning: "Never illegally dispose of your garbage. This is STRICTLY PROHIBITED by law." I for one certainly do not want to go to prison for not separating my trash!

Basically, garbage is divided into "recyclable" and "non-recyclable" categories. Twice a month, we are allowed to put out "cans" and "bottles." The cans must be divided between aluminum, steel and regular metal cans. Spray cans must be pierced with something to release the gas. The picture shows a man using a hammer and nail to puncture the can, which scares the dickens out of me, so I usually forego this little step.

The bottles must be separated by colors: colorless, brown and "other" colors. These should only be food and drink bottles (other types are disposed on another day in a totally different category). The caps on the bottles are placed in the category called "miscellaneous" plastics.

Once a month, cartons and cardboard boxes are picked up. Milk and juice cartons must be washed, dried and cut so that they lay flat.

Cardboard boxes must be flattened and bundled using "paper-based" cord. Twice a month, we are allowed to dispose of "miscellaneous paper" (paper bags, gift and/or tissue boxes—the plastic strip must be removed from the top of the tissue box, however, and placed in "miscellaneous plastics"). Also, "clear recyclable plastic bottles" are picked up twice a month and these include water, soft drink, juice and tea containers that can be recycled.

Because Japan has a tendency to "over-package" most everything that is food-related, "miscellaneous plastics" are picked up once a week. It is amazing how much trash is generated by a typical family of four in Japan. These plastics include anything other than the recyclable bottles, like instant noodle cups, potato chip bags, shampoo bottles, egg cartons, and even the childproof medication packages where the medicine is punched through the cellophane backing. These do not include, however, toothpaste tubes which must be disposed with "non-burnable refuse."

Twice a month, items such as pots, pans, plastic toys, light bulbs, shoes, batteries, ceramics, and buckets are picked up. Once a month, really big items are picked up, including wooden furniture, small heaters, bicycles, old carpets, spring mattresses, and steel items like bookshelves, beds and desks. Thankfully, twice a week the city picks up burnable refuse which is the "wet" garbage from cooking; also, old clothes, stuffed animals, twigs and garden clippings, and anything that can be burned cleanly and that which is not included in any of the other categories.

I have developed quite a system for sorting all of these items into small bags that are placed in larger trash cans outside. In my neighborhood, trash days occur from Tuesday through Friday, and the garbage must be put out on the day, not before 6:00 am and not after 9:00 am.

In the early morning, I stumble down to the trash collection site at the crack of dawn, bags in hand, to do my nearly daily trash ritual. It is a good time to greet neighbors, though, who are doing the same. Sometimes several of us have an impromptu *idobatakaigi* (literally "meeting around the well") which is basically a "gossip session."

This catches me up on what is going on in the neighborhood, and ensures that they are not talking about me. A recent topic was how "someone" was not using the required "clear" trash bags for the recyclable and the "green" trash bags for the burnable trash. Of course, I feigned shock at this revelation (knowing that I have been known to mix bag colors from time to time when in a pinch). It worked. Everyone was satisfied with my seeming surprise at such atrocious behavior.

[37] *Living in Japan's Snow Country Means Shoveling a lot of Snow*

Aomori, the prefecture where I live in Japan, is located at the northernmost tip of the main island of Honshu. This region of the country is notorious for its incredible winters and huge snow accumulations. In normal years, snow begins to fall in mid-December and does not stop until late March. It is not at all uncommon to get a foot of snow in a day. In one 24 hour period a few years ago we received nearly a yard of snow.

It seems unbelievable, but it is just a fact of life here in "snow country." Each morning, everyone gets out and shovels the snow in front of their homes, piling it in every available space in the yard and around the house. *Yuki kaki* or "snow removal" is the obligation of homeowners. There are no sidewalks, so often homes are built nearly on the street. Everyone clears away the snow from in front of their own home, which is basically the public street. My particular street is much too narrow to have a snowplow come down, so it is up to us to get out early and shovel away the snow before people begin to go to work and children walk to school.

Most cars here have front wheel drive and no one seems at all bothered by the snow, plowing through as if it was not there. A fraction of this amount of snow would bring most cities in other countries to a complete standstill.

American school children will be disappointed to hear that there is no concept of "snow days" here where school is canceled. In fact, in all the years I have lived here, I have never heard of anything being canceled due to snow, with the exception of some flights and trains because of drifting snow. School is held regardless because there is no school busing system here like in the United States; students must walk, take public transportation, or be driven by a parent each day to school.

Snow is piled in every available space during the height of winter in "snow country"

One interesting sight during the winter season is seeing old men determined to ride their bikes on packed snow and ice no matter what. They ride, teeter-tottering along the road, doing whatever they can to keep the bike from slipping out from under them. Where they are going, I have no idea, but it is amazing that they even attempt such an outing.

Sadly, every year, a number people die due to the snow, mostly being buried alive from trying to remove the snow off the roofs of their homes. One woman was killed when she fell into a creek; she was pushing snow from near her home into the waterway when she lost her footing and fell in. A number of children perish each year when it begins to warm up, causing huge chunks of snow to avalanche off the roofs of homes onto where they are playing below. Japanese parents do their best to warn children not to play below the roofs, but kids will be kids. Also, sometimes roofs cave in due to the weight of the snow, covering those inside with a mixture of snow and rubble.

Men performing "snow removal" off a roof after an especially heavy snowfall

My roof has small "snow stoppers" every so many feet to keep the snow from sliding off in one huge chunk. It makes it safer for those on the ground, but means the weight of the snow stays on the roof. The extreme weight of the snow makes it very dangerous for older homes. Every year a number of homes are damaged and even completely destroyed by the weight of the snow. It is common practice here to hire snow removal people to climb onto the roof to push off the accumulated snow. I had a difficult time finding someone to do it one year when we had an especially large accumulation of snow. They were all booked solid for weeks because so many homes were in need of being cleared of snow.

That same year, one prefecture had to have the Self Defense Forces assist residents in a mountain village get the snow off their roofs. The news showed one house literally buried. When they finally got the front door dug out, a very grateful old man came out to thank them. Some years the snow is so heavy on my roof that the upstairs' bedroom doors wedge shut. This was a serious problem, because the beams in my attic buckled causing cracks to form in the plasterboard on my walls due to the weight of the snow.

Luckily, I had recently had my home earthquake-proofed which gave it extra strength, but it was still damaged nonetheless. So, I am quite aware of how much snow is on my roof at any one time, and I tend to get it cleared off before it gets to be a yard or so high after settling.

A neighbor two doors down always has snow up past the first floor of the house. Every November, they put slats of wood across the windows so when the snow starts to pile up the pressure from the snow does not break through into the house itself. They have just enough space to get in and out of the house through the front door.

It all seems so dreadful, I know, but I actually do not mind the snowy weather. It keeps me active, giving me plenty of daily exercise, and frequent opportunities to talk to my neighbors. It certainly is a communal effort to keep the snow at bay.

[38] *Bowing to the Porcelain God—Japan's Toilet Culture*

Before my mother's first trip to Japan many, many years ago, one main concern I had with her visit had nothing to do with her not being able to use chopsticks, eat the food, speak the language, or climb the countless stairs to take the trains and subways—I worried about being able to secure appropriate toilet facilities, acceptable enough for my mother's discerning tastes, at all the points of interest we were scheduled to visit.

I even went as far as to scout out places before her arrival in order to make sure proper facilities were available. Fortunately, today, this type of concern is largely unfounded as the vast majority of public restrooms are now clean and modern, often being equipped with at least one Western-style toilet.

When I first arrived in Japan, however, this was not the case. Many public toilets were not connected to sewage systems, which meant the stench was staggering, especially during the height of summer; also, the vast majority of toilets were the traditional "squat" type of toilet that required a certain amount of dexterity and stamina, not to mention balance, to accomplish the given task at hand.

Western tourists who visit Japan often have a fear (unfounded in my opinion) of using a Japanese-style toilet. To be honest, I prefer the traditional toilets because they are much cleaner and healthier to use than the common Western-style chair-type toilets. With squat toilets, at no time does one's body ever touch any part of the toilet, so the user avoids any potentially unhygienic contact with a surface someone else has just touched or used.

A traditional "squat" toilet in a public restroom

When a dear friend of mine from home came to visit me in Japan, she proudly proclaimed as we prepared to leave for Tokyo at the end of her visit that she had successfully avoided using a Japanese-style toilet throughout her entire two-week visit. Her jubilant proclamation was a bit premature. The overnight sleeper we took to Tokyo, an older style train, was only equipped with traditional squat-type toilets. The train ride is around 12 hours long. You do the math.

My friend finally could not wait any longer and decided she had to venture into the toilet car to do her business. How she did it, I have no idea, but she claimed she was able to use the squat toilet without squatting…which means she must have used the toilet standing up. This is all the more amazing when considering she did this on a moving train, which requires even more skill because the train is constantly swaying back and forth. Luckily, a handlebar is located on both sides so users can steady themselves while using it on a moving train.

Generally speaking, toilets in Japan have certainly come a long way since the early days when the Western-style toilet was first introduced. In many ways, the Japanese chair-type toilet has now surpassed in comfort and styles those of the West. One unique feature that is standard on most toilets here are water saving measures. The flush mechanism allows the user to choose between a powerful or a weaker flush, depending upon what is being flushed. Also, on top of the tank is a sink where the water that is used to fill the tank is first utilized by the user to wash his/her hands before it drains into the tank to be recycled. This same water is then used for the next flush.

One common practice here amongst women is the habit of repeatedly flushing a toilet over and over while tinkling. A Japanese woman is much too modest to risk having someone hear her using the toilet. So, the water saving measure (incorporated into the design of the toilet) was rendered meaningless. Not to fear. Japan with all of its innovative ingenuity came up with a workable solution—piping in the sound of running water into women's toilets via speakers loud enough to muffle any individual sounds.

Another gadget that was widely installed in women's toilets was a push button system that mimicked the sound of a flushing toilet, used at the discretion of the user. This solved the problem of having gallons upon gallons of water being wastefully flushed down the toilet. Women could tinkle with the reassurance of knowing that no one could hear what they were doing.

In the past few years, public toilets have gotten very swanky in many respects. It is not at all uncommon to find toilets with built in "washlet" or bidet systems which allow users to wash their undersides after using the toilet, with an extra setting exclusively for women. Many elderly people here, however, would rather not have all the bells and whistles, preferring the simple squat toilet. But, modern technology has forced them, in a pinch, to use the newfangled contraptions. Nearly always, thankfully, directions with an illustration are posted on the wall featuring stick figures properly using the Western-style toilet for those who may not be familiar or comfortable with the concept.

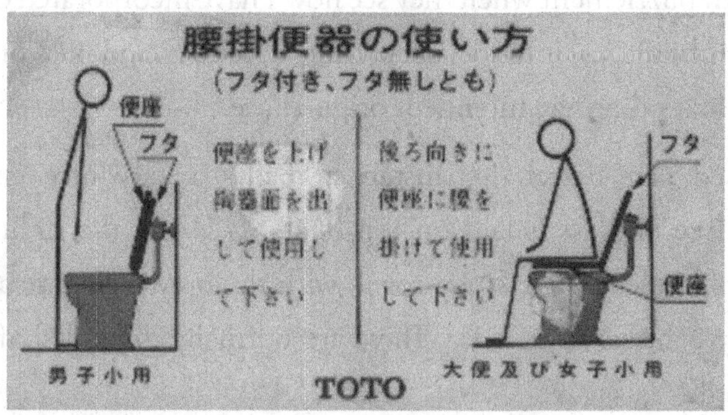

Illustrated instructions on how to properly use a Western-style toilet

One luxury that I cannot live without and one which most of you may think is frivolous is the "heated" toilet seat. Living in snow country, without the luxury of central heating, means that the toilet area is not heated. Believe me, it is not an extravagance. On visits home, that initial shock one's bottom receives when sitting on a cold toilet seat reminds me of how wonderful this little invention truly is. Once you have experienced the joy of a heated toilet seat, a normal toilet seat is quite meager in comparison.

[39] *Traditional Japanese Objects as Home Decorating Accessories*

Sometimes when Japanese people visit my home, they scratch their heads with puzzlement when they see how I have incorporated everyday Japanese objects as interior decorating accents...and in completely different ways than the intended, original use.

A used *sake* barrel, for instance, makes a very nice end table once a piece of glass is laid on top of it. It is just the right height, wrapped in a decorative straw cover, with the brewer's name and logo colorfully painted all over it. These are normally discarded after they are opened.

People who arrive at my home in Japan are greeted by a smiling figure of *Kintaro* (a popular character in Japanese folklore) peering out of the window. From outside, everyone thinks it is stained glass, but in fact it is a traditional banner I have hanging in my stairway that goes from the second-floor ceiling all the way to the bottom landing of the stairs. His face just happens to be positioned in the window when viewed from outside, but from inside, it is a stunning interior accent that is normally only used during festivals. Also, as guests climb my stairs, I have a child's *kimono* hanging on the wall. It is 100% silk with an embroidered scene of a warrior in full armor.

A beautiful *obi* (*kimono* sash) adorns the top of a long cabinet I have in my upstairs hallway. The width is perfect, and of course, the fabric is exquisite. When older ladies visiting my home realize it is an *obi*, they are usually shocked, then fascinated in how it is being utilized. Again, few if any Japanese would use what they consider to be clothing as decorative objects. Recently, I purchased an *obi* that I will use in my home in the US. My idea is to drape it on a long rod near the ceiling in such a way that shows not only the embroidered side, but also the plain side. To my eyes, the plain side is as beautiful as the decorative side.

A *kimono* sash, *obi*, is used as a decorative runner on a cabinet

There is a local shop here where I always take friends and family who visit me. The owner is accustomed to my frequent visits bringing a gaggle of foreigners in to browse around her constantly changing stock. It is a recycle shop for Japanese *kimonos* and accessories. I am sure she is amused by the types of articles we buy, wondering how we can possibly wear them. Unbeknownst to her, no one ever intends to wear the items; some of the *kimonos* will be hung in living rooms, some *obis* used in dining rooms as table runners, others cut up and made into pillow covers.

When my cousins visited, we went to her shop and bought several items. Once they returned home, they decided they really wanted a beautiful, white wedding *kimono* that she had displayed. So, I went back to the shop. Amazingly, it was still there, so I proceeded to purchase it. She was quite confused as to why I was buying a woman's wedding *kimono*. She did remember my cousins and how enamored they were with this item, so I told her that it was for them and that they wanted it to display in their home as a wall-hanging. I am sure she had a difficult time envisioning how a wedding *kimono* could be hung on a wall; in her mind's eye, it would look quite out of place. Everywhere I look, though, I see a potential interior object.

In Japan, once a month, we have a *sodai gomi* day which is for discarding large trash items. I know that some foreigners in big cities get up very early to ride their bikes up and down the narrow streets to see what items have been thrown out. Often, a nice antique piece of furniture can be found in the pile of trash. One person's trash is certainly another person's treasure.

Japanese people do not have the custom of garage or rummage sales to get rid of unwanted items. If the item cannot be sold to a recycle shop, often people will throw perfectly good things out on *sodai gomi* day. I certainly am guilty of doing this. I always ask around to see if a neighbor or student may want the item I no longer need, but normally I have to carry it down to the trash heap because no one I know wants it.

In the past few years, perhaps due to the bad economy that has plagued Japan for the past two decades, there has been an interest in selling used items at flea markets (called "free" markets here). The city will sponsor these throughout the year, and people can reserve a space and sell items they no longer need. Popular among young people is clothing.

A teacher-friend of mine once gave a *furoshiki* to my mother as a gift. This is a traditional square cloth that is used to wrap and carry items. It is used like a bag, in essence, but is elegant and beautiful in its simplicity. The patterns on these are quite stunning; some are made of silk, others cotton, and yet some are synthetic. They are exclusively used here to carry things.

When I told my teacher-friend that my mother liked it so much that she decided to wear it as a scarf, the look of horror on her face was priceless. People utilize these to carry objects from one place to another—never wear them. A Japanese woman would never wear one around her neck because people would think she was touched in the head. It would be akin to an American woman wearing a Wal-Mart bag on her head—something that might happen if she is caught in a deluge without an umbrella and needs to dart from the car to the house, but never as a fashion statement…or at least I hope not.

[40] *US Star Power gives way to Korean Heartthrob in Japan*

Often people outside Japan are curious about what famous foreign stars and entertainers are popular here. It is a well known fact that a number of A-list stars who would never consider doing a commercial in the West are quite happy to come to Japan to cash in on their fame by peddling anything from soap to cars. In particular, American entertainers and sports celebrities have created a cottage industry for themselves earning extra cash by coming over here to do Japanese commercials.

In the past, this was a very lucrative part-time job for big name American stars. As featured in the movie, *Lost in Translation*, a fading film star (played by Bill Murray) was in Japan to make some quick cash by hawking whiskey in print and television ads. He was beyond bored with the whole idea. Soon he became frustrated with the subtleties of Japanese culture and with doing business in Japan, of which he had absolutely no clue.

In the past, this was certainly a very representative scenario of how US celebrities would fly in for a few days, say a couple of words in English for a commercial, then fly home with s suitcase bulging with cash—millions of dollars in some cases. These stars, however, had iron-clad contracts which restricted the use of the advertisement to the Japanese market only. The ads or commercials could not be used outside of Japan.

The reason for this was largely cultural to a certain degree. In the United States, traditionally, stars that would do commercials were labeled "has-beens." Their careers waning (their popularity at an all time low) would be forced to take what they could get in the form of work, so commercials were sometimes their only options. I remember seeing a celebrity who was formerly quite famous selling windows on late night TV and thinking, "Poor guy—he just doesn't have it anymore." It was an attitude of pity.

The author with Korean superstar, Bae Yong Jun…or at least a cardboard cutout of the heartthrob

In Japan, the opposite is true. The hottest stars and entertainers are regularly featured in the trendiest commercials for ultimate exposure to the public. I suppose the US equivalent would be for an American agent to parade an actor on the talk-show circuit to promote a new project or movie.

On recent trips home, I have noticed a big change in this area. More and more "A-list" stars are gladly accepting gigs on commercials and in print ads. Perhaps they have realized that instead of signaling there demise from show business, a well-placed commercial could actually be a catalyst to bigger and better things in the industry. That certainly is the case in Japan.

Sadly for US stars, though, the trend in Japan recently is not to feature American celebrities as much as other Asian entertainers. There has been a real upheaval in the market here and people are crazy for Korean, Hong Kong, Chinese and Thai entertainers. One of the biggest of these stars is a Korean man called "Yon-sama" (his character's name) who has taken the country by storm. He was featured in a public television program imported from Korea several years ago called *Winter Sonata*. He has had more staying power than most. I have seen many famous faces come and go over the years. This program, however, was an unexpected and wildly popular hit with middle-aged to elderly women, keeping them glued to their TV sets every Sunday night. The result was a "Korea boom" that was unprecedented in the history of Korean-Japanese relations. Historically, relations between Japan and Korea have been rocky at best. Even the 2002 World Cup that was shared between these two neighboring nations as a way to bridge diplomatic relations did nothing in comparison to what Bae Yong Jun (Yon-sama's real name) did in his romantic portrayal of a love struck boy involved in a love triangle.

Interest in this imported Korean soap opera was so great that tourism to Korea exploded—fans rushed to Korea to see the house and scenes featured in the drama. Travel agencies designed tours to cater to these women who could not get enough of "Yon-sama." In fact, middle-aged women wept, screamed, and even fainted when the actor came to Japan on a promotional tour. There were so many fifty-something women fans at the Tokyo airport to greet him that security guards had to usher him out a back door for fear that some of these women might get trampled if the riotous mob pushed forward for a closer look. Trust me…one does not want to be involved in a stampede of middle-aged

Japanese women delirious with a longing desire for a fantasy romance with a television character.

I have to admit, I was a bit curious about the hoopla surrounding this Korean-phenomenon called Yon-sama, so I took a trip to Korea to see for myself. I can report that he is every bit as big in Korea as he is in Japan. Even the duty-free emporium had an entire store devoted to goods with his likeness emblazoned on everything from dainty socks to chunky ashtrays. He is a business unto himself and anyone and everyone is jumping on his coattails in hopes of getting a piece of the pie. Street vendors selling his likeness on trinkets and knickknacks are making a bundle with the Japanese tourists who grab up everything related to him.

So, instead of US movie stars gracing all the print ads in magazines, and being featured in all the prime-time TV commercials, a new trend in Japan is everything Asian. And the Japanese cannot get enough! That one soap-opera, *Winter Sonata*, and the actor, Bae Yong Jun, did more towards normalizing diplomatic relations between Korea and Japan than all of the politicians, diplomats, and sports exchanges combined. Now, that is impressive.

[41] *Japan, a Safe Country? Yes and No*

"Japan is a safe country." Generally speaking, this statement is true when comparing Japan to most other countries. In fact, Tokyo, one of the world's largest cities, is quite safe when compared to other big cities around the planet.

For instance, when walking down a dark street in Tokyo alone, I never feel anxious or uneasy about walking late at night in an unfamiliar area. However, as soon as I get to Europe or North America, I have my guard up. I am much more aware of others around me, even in places I know well.

Not long ago, a British friend and I were walking down a narrow street in Tokyo when a group of leather clad teens—with punked-out pink and green spiked-hair, dressed menacingly with skulls and crossbones on their jackets, adorned with chunky chains as fashion accessories—came strutting toward us. Neither of us flinched or even paid them any mind at all except to comment that if we had been in London or New York, and a gang of boys approached dressed in a similar fashion, we both would have been on high alert, vigilantly eyeing their every move.

This sense of security when traveling or living in Japan is one of its greatest assets for not only Japanese people but for foreign visitors as well. Random crimes against foreigners are virtually unheard of here, making Japan a popular travel destination, especially for women. The low crime rate in Japan may be attributed to its Confucian ideals found in Buddhism and in its own indigenous religion of *Shinto*. Throughout Japanese history, *Shinto* and Buddhist beliefs advocating non-violence have been a cornerstone of its religious and "moral" education.

During the Tokugawa Shogunate (1603-1867) *samurai* warriors were in charge of keeping the peace and did so with iron hands. Reportedly, they were even permitted to execute people on the spot for minor infractions like impoliteness or breaking the law for things that people in modern society routinely do with impunity. This history and tradition has translated into a modern society that is largely honest and law-abiding. When I first arrived in Japan, I had to watch myself at crosswalks because I would sometimes cross when it was red and there were no cars in sight; Japanese people, on the other hand, will stand and wait until the walk sign lights up. I do not want to be a bad influence, so I now wait until the light turns before crossing.

Drivers here, though, do run red-lights as a matter of course. The opposite light stays red for a couple of extra seconds to allow the stragglers to get through before the other light turns green. This is a definite no-no in most other countries. Many a ticket has been issued to such drivers for running a red light. In Japan, it is expected and everyone does it.

Samurai of the Satsuma Clan during the Boshin War Period[6]

Japan is notorious for having mislaid or forgotten items on trains returned to the person who lost them. I have left the occasional bag or odd umbrella (or two) in a taxi or on a bus or train; each time I was able to get my belongings back because some Good Samaritan took the item to the lost-and-found office or gave it to the driver.

I always warn my students who are visiting a foreign country for the first time to be vigilant and careful because they are not used to worrying about scam artists, conmen, or thieves who might take advantage of their naïveté as novice travelers. Routinely in Japan, as a matter of course, Japanese people will board a train, place their bag or briefcase on a shelf above their seat, and promptly fall asleep. When they reach the station where they want to get off, they jump up and grab their belongings, then head out the door. The entire time they are riding on the train they appear to be asleep (or at least playing possum). You cannot do this in most other large cities around the world. Your bag most likely will not be there when you wake up. So, I try to give my students some simple, but smart travel tips before they leave.

In Japan, it is common for Japanese travelers to find an empty seat at a train station or in an airport to leave their bags while they do some last minute shopping, use a public phone, or go to the toilet. Again, this is unwise in other countries because someone will probably see it and take it. Also, with terrorism on everyone's mind, others may be suspicious of an unattended bag sitting alone on a seat in a public place.

I also caution my students not to venture into unknown parts at night or alone when abroad. It is fun and adventurous to explore new places, but they have to be smart about it and research the area and go to places where there are a lot of people around. This is the reality of traveling abroad in most places other than Japan. This is not to say, however, that Japan is "crime-free" because it is not. It is rarer here, and when someone is attacked, or worse, murdered, it makes national headlines. A disturbing trend that has been occurring more frequently is crimes against children who are abducted and often killed.

Youth generated crime has increased at an alarming rate in the last several years. Once unheard of, it is now becoming more and more frequent. A number of years ago, a boy killed his classmate, severed the head, and placed it at the front gate of his school. More recently, a young boy kidnapped a toddler from a store where the parents were shopping, took him to a parking garage, mutilated the toddler's genitalia, and then threw him over the side.

This rash of violent crimes committed by children against children has been in the news more habitually in recent years here. Of course, similar heinous crimes against children elsewhere are almost commonplace to the point where people are desensitized to it when it does happen. In Japan, it is still rare enough that the media is right on it and it causes the nation collectively to gasp in horror.

The authorities here, as well as educators, are trying to understand why this disturbing trend is happening. Like most first-world countries that are industrialized and wealthy, the rapid transformation of Japan regarding its social attitudes, standard of living, and culture has outpaced the ability of society to digest the changes in a way that teaches its youth a sense of propriety, giving them a social conscience to know right from wrong.

Sadly, it happened in the West, and I fear it is happening here.

[42] *Death Related Superstitions in Japan*

Every culture has superstitions that are embedded into its peoples' psyches. Western cultures certainly have many superstitions. Whether it is "knocking on wood" for good luck or "blessing" another person who sneezes, we often unconsciously adhere to certain superstitions that have been passed down from generation to generation.

Japan is no different. Many of America's superstitions were brought to its shores by immigrants from much older cultures; Japan's superstitions, on the other hand, are largely homegrown, in some cases dating back to time immemorial.

For instance, few Americans would ever dare walk under a ladder for fear of creating bad luck for themselves. Do you know where this superstition comes from? Most likely, this superstition probably originated in medieval Europe when people were regularly hanged to death as a punishment for serious crimes. The condemned was forced to walk under a ladder when taken to the gallows where the hanging took place; the executioner then would climb the same ladder to cut the noose after the execution. For obvious reasons, people were a bit squeamish about walking under a ladder due to this ominous association. Death, and superstitions related to death, has prominence in most cultures.

Likewise, but for entirely different reasons, Japan has a wide variety of "death" related superstitions. These are quite different from Western ones, but equally important in that the majority of Japanese people adhere to these naturally and often unconsciously.

One example has to do with passing food from person-to-person using chopsticks. A Japanese person would never do this under any circumstance. And if it were ever done unwittingly by foreign visitors in the presence of a Japanese national, I am sure the Japanese person would gasp out loud in utter horror. The polite way to give someone a bite of your food is to first invert the chopsticks (using the ends that have not touched your mouth) and gently place the offered food onto a small plate for the other person.

The only time that Japanese people ever have the occasion to pass anything from chopstick to chopstick is at a cremation ceremony for someone who has died. After the body is cremated, family and close friends congregate around the skeletal remains and ashes to assist in collecting the vestiges of the deceased person. The closest family members, using disposable chopsticks, pick up the skull, pelvic bone, arms, and legs together to place them in an ornate box. Each person present then takes a turn to pick up a remaining bone to place it reverently into the box.

Most people outside of Japan are unaware that a cremated person's bones do not burn, but are largely intact when the body is pulled from the cremation oven. Later, crematoriums pulverize the bones, mixing them with the ashes from the body and wooden casket. In Japan, the bones are never crushed, but gathered up and preserved as they are. This Japanese custom of gathering a loved one's bones after the cremation is called *watashibashi*. Hence, the only time someone exchanges something with another directly with chopsticks in Japan is at a funeral.

Sometimes foreigners in Japan commit another huge social *faux pas* by sticking their chopsticks into a bowl of rice instead of resting them politely on the edge of the bowl horizontally. Again, this breach of proper Japanese etiquette is also directly related to death because a bowl of rice that is offered to the soul of the dead at a Buddhist funeral is prepared in this way. This rice is called *makurameshi.*

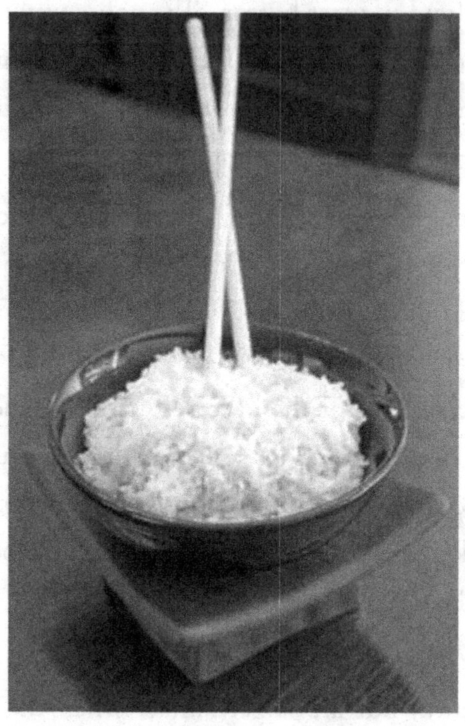

Makurameshi, "chopsticks in a bowl of rice," should never be done outside of a Buddhist altar or funeral ceremony

Unintentionally, sometimes foreign visitors offend Japanese diners by casually sticking their chopsticks upright in a bowl of rice without knowing the social protocol and cultural implications of doing such a thing. Needless to say, doing this will bring dinner conversation to a screeching halt, leaving the clueless foreigner wondering what just happened.

I found myself trying to understand a similar situation when I rented my first apartment in Japan. I had purchased a bed and when it was delivered, the delivery personnel were quite worried about its placement in the bedroom. Before they would even bring the bed into the room, the two men went out onto the balcony, craned their necks to see where the sun was, had a short confabulation, then came in and gave me a "thumbs up."

I was thoroughly confused as to why it would make a difference where the bed was placed in the room. Little did I know, in Japan, it is very bad luck to sleep with your head to the north. Again, this is a death-related superstition that all Japanese know and follow—just like Westerners would have reservation about opening an umbrella in the house or be perturbed if a black cat crossed their path.

In Japan, a corpse is always laid out with the head to the north. This is called *kitamakura* in Japanese. Luckily for the delivery people, I wanted the headboard on the south wall, making everyone happy. I am sure they were shocked initially when they arrived because I lived on the fourth floor.

The pronunciation of the number four in Japanese is *shi* which also sounds like "death." Often, Japanese hospitals or high-rise buildings avoid having floors or rooms numbered "four" because of this association (just like some buildings in the West do not have a 13th floor). I, of course, was none-the-wiser when I moved into the apartment building on the fourth floor. Interestingly, though, for the longest time there were no other tenants on my floor until the entire rest of the building had filled up and only fourth-floor apartments were available. Although the superstitions between the West and Japan are quite different based on cultural, religious, and historical considerations, both have similar intentions in trying to avoid any potentially unlucky situations.

Of course, superstitions concerning numbers are quite plentiful in both cultures. Few Westerners fail to notice a "Friday the 13th." Japanese people also have superstitions related to numbers; as I mentioned earlier, the number "four" has an ominous meaning in Japan because it is pronounced the same as the word for "death" in Japanese.

Just as hospitals and high-rises sometimes avoid using the number "13" for floor and room numbers in America, a similar custom is followed in Japan with regards to the number "4." The reason why Western cultures avoid the number "13" is connected to Christianity. It comes from the Last Supper that Jesus held before his trial and crucifixion; there were 13 who attended, and Judas, who betrayed Jesus, was among them.

Christians always refer to the "12" disciples of Jesus and even today most place settings for formal dinners come in sets of 12. It is unlucky to have 13 guests at one's table. The same is true in Japan in that it is impossible to find a set of "4" of anything—plates, glasses, cutlery, etc. Most everything in Japan comes in sets of "five" to avoid the unlucky "four" connection.

Also, in Japan, the number "9" is considered unlucky in hospitals because it is pronounced the same as the word for "pain" (*ku*). Many Japanese superstitions related to numbers come from a type of double entendre or pun in the pronunciation of the word.

The lucky number "7" has Biblical roots as well for Western cultures. Jews and Christians believe that God created the heavens and the earth in six days and rested on the seventh; Noah's rainbow had seven colors; there are seven sins—pride, wrath, envy, lust, gluttony, avarice, and laziness; Salome performed a dance of the seven veils; and the Beast of the Apocalypse has seven heads. The number seven, hence, is also closely related to religion. The number "7" was highly significant in Jewish religious tradition because it represented perfection and signified completeness. Christians adopted this belief of viewing the number "7" as being auspicious as well.

Since July 7, 2007 fell on a Saturday—7-7-07—there were many couples who married on this day because of its lucky implications. As well, casinos were brimming with customers that year on July 7th in the hope that the lucky day will somehow translate into big winnings. Likewise, Japanese people also regard the number "7" as being lucky. Perhaps the modern connotation of this superstition was imported to Japan from the West, but Japan does have a tradition of viewing the number "7" as "lucky."

For instance, in Buddhism, there are the "Seven Gods of Good Luck"—*Benten* (goddess of love), *Bishamon* (god of war), *Daitoku* (god of wealth), *Ebisu* (god of modesty), *Fukurokuju* and *Jurojin* (gods of long-life), and *Hotei* (god of merriment). A clever American friend of mine started a wine-import company here and named it "Hotei" which is one of the seven gods of good luck. It is quite successful and ever-expanding.

The traditional six-day Buddhist calendar, imported from China in the 14th century and practiced in Japan from the mid-Edo Period (1600-1868), still makes modern people superstitious about certain days considered to be auspicious and others which are regarded as being very unlucky.

The six day calendar (*rokuyo*) is divided as *taian*, *butsumetsu*, *sempu*, *tomobiki*, *shako*, and *sensho*. The luckiest of the six days is *taian* and Japanese people will often seal business deals on this day and many engaged couples choose to marry on this day. *Butsumetsu* is considered to be a very unlucky day; hence people avoid doing anything important on this day. If possible, Japanese people try not to have a loved one's funeral held on *tomobiki* because it is believed that the deceased person may try to bring the living to the underworld, or by having a funeral on this day will invite another death soon after.

Every year in December, many businesses like banks and taxi companies will give out calendars to their customers. Many of these calendars feature these fortunes. An example of a fortune is: "*Sempu*—Urgent business and controversy should be avoided on this day. It is a good day for going about other activities in a serene manner. The afternoon is auspicious." Just as many Westerners will read their daily horoscope, I am sure that a goodly number of Japanese people make a point to check their calendar each day to see if it is an auspicious or inauspicious day facing them. If it happens to be a *butsumetsu* day then the whole day will be anxious and tense; but if it happens to be a *taian* day, then the person will most likely be happy and at ease.

[43] *Sumo Wrestling More than a Sport, it's a Living Treasure*

Several years ago when a friend from home visited me, it happened to be during one of the regularly scheduled "*Sumo* Grand Tournaments." Each day she sat mesmerized in front of the television, watching with great anticipation who would win the bout and who would ultimately lose. Just after a few days, she had figured out the rules and was rooting for her favorite players. This reaction to *sumo* wrestling is typical of visitors to Japan. There is something very absorbing about the national sport of Japan that hooks people after just a couple of hours of watching it.

Each new season brings a grand tournament which packs the stadium where the bouts are held, and has office workers huddled around their office televisions to watch the outcomes of the bouts of the higher ranked wrestlers. Although the bouts usually last a matter of seconds, it is very exciting to watch. Part of the attraction is the history of the sport, dating back some 2,000 years. It is highly ritualized, reflecting an aesthetic art form of ancient Japan that has been passed down over the millennia, retaining many of the same aspects and traditions today as it did then.

Japanese people absolutely love *sumo* and consider it to be a living national treasure. The top wrestlers who reach the rank of *yokozuna* are treated like superstars. Magazine and television advertisements feature the popular wrestlers. Memorabilia, similar to other sports, feature wrestlers' likenesses on towels, cards, posters, t-shirts and any other imaginable type of souvenir. Unlike most sports, however, *sumo*-stardom brings with it a huge social and cultural responsibility that is steeped in tradition and proper etiquette that dates back to its beginning. Having dignity and respect for the sport, and what it stands for, is of utmost importance to the wrestlers…and to the spectators.

No matter how strong or powerful a wrestler is, without a certain air of dignity that is associated with champion wrestlers of the highest rank, a wrestler will not be promoted to the rank of *yokozuna*. This is what sets *sumo* apart from other major sports around the world. A wrestler's success is not solely dependent upon his ability, but on the whole package of how he is able to conduct himself with respect to *sumo* and its long history of codified rituals; all of this is in addition to his adroitness in the ring.

Sumo is considered to be a "living museum" of a bygone era because of its rituals and traditions. In some ways, it is more of a performance than a sport. A fan is transported during each bout to a time that is reminiscent of Edo Period Japan (1600-1868). In the 15th century, *sumo* wrestlers were used to help train *samurai*. To fall in battle meant instant death, so to muster the strength and dignity to get up after falling was an embodiment of the *sumo* ethic, one that served *samurai* warriors well. Conquering physical exhaustion, staying on your feet no matter what, and getting up after falling are lessons that are still taught to young *sumo* wrestlers today.

Sumo practice is hard. Wrestlers' entire lives and daily routines are centered on *sumo*. They eat, breathe and sleep *sumo* during the entire time they are training and wrestling, just as their predecessors have done for hundreds of years. A wrestler's day begins at 4:00 or 5:00 am for the youngest or lowest ranked wrestlers. They must ready the ring for the day's practice and exercise to get loosened up for the pummeling they will most certainly endure from the higher ranked wrestlers. Physically, the young wrestlers must learn balance, flexibility, and agility—the three essentials for success in the *sumo* ring. The goal is to have extremely powerful thighs and a very low center of gravity.

When most people think of *sumo*, the image is of gargantuan men with neatly combed topknots, stomping their feet one at a time from a high position. This exercise is called *shiko* and young wrestlers do this at least 500 times a day. They also sit with their legs spread far apart, leaning down until their stomach and face touch the ring...not an easy feat to achieve with a huge belly of fat in the way. Not to fear, older wrestlers help the younger ones by standing on their backs to help get the needed flexibility—a painful, but effective technique.

In time immemorial, legend has it that territorial disputes were sometimes settled through *sumo* bouts. The "will" of the gods decided the outcome, so people would accept success or defeat. This is a more peaceful and less bloody way to settle disputes; much better than the "shock and awe" methods of modern warfare today.

Why do *sumo* wrestlers wear the stylized-topknot? The hairstyle actually serves two purposes: 1) it is to help protect the wrestler's head from injury; and 2) it symbolizes the sanctity of the sport and his position within the world of *sumo*. In fact, the people in charge of coiffing the hair of a *sumo* wrestler have to train for years before being allowed to touch the hair of a top-ranked wrestler. Apprenticeship of the traditional arts of Japan, including *sumo*, is a time-honored tradition with generations of family members often performing the same function as their ancestors.

The unique style of a *sumo* wrestler's topknot is significant because the hairdresser must mold and shape the hair, applying copious amounts of oil, into the shape of a ginkgo leaf. This style is reserved for only the top-ranked wrestlers to don before matches. If a lower-ranked wrestler goes out of his stable building into the public, he is always expected to wear *kimono* with *geta* (wooden clogs) and have his hair tied in a topknot called *chommage* (if it is long enough) which was typical of men in the Edo Period.

As mentioned before, only the top-ranked wrestlers are allowed to have their hair oiled and combed in the *oichomage* (gingko leaf) style during tournaments. Once a top-ranked wrestler retires, there is a special "haircutting" ceremony that takes place in the ring. The wrestler, dressed in formal *kimono*, sits in the center of the ring as family, friends, fellow wrestlers, and celebrities who are fans take turns in snipping bits of his hair. This is a very emotional ceremony, and often the wrestlers are not able to hold back the wave of emotion that engulfs them at having such a visible part of their *sumo* identity taken away from them.

Before every Grand *Sumo* Tournament, a new *dohyo* (ring) is made by hand by a legion of 40 specialists for four days. The *dohyo* is considered to be a sacred place—a meeting ground for the gods—and only a select group of men are allowed to construct the ring before a tournament. It takes one ten years of training just to be able to choose the proper clay to use in the making of a *sumo* ring.

By hand, using only traditional tools—just as it was done 2,000 years ago—packed earth and the hard work of the 40 specialists combine to make a good *dohyo*. These men are called *yobidashi*, or beckoner/usher, who besides making the *dohyo* also beckon the wrestlers for their bouts and who usher them into the stadium. They serve as referees, as well, for the bouts.

Yobidashi begin their training at the age of 15 and spend their whole lives honing their ability to create a perfect ring, and in becoming a "master *yobidashi*." These men assist in all aspects of the *sumo* matches from keeping the ring moist with water to prevent it from cracking, to sweeping the loosened earth from the center, to handing sweat towels to the wrestlers before and after their matches. They are also responsible for carrying the huge advertising banners of sponsors around the ring before the matches.

Akebono at his retirement ceremony[7]

Sumo is rapidly becoming an international sport. Occasionally, exhibition matches are performed and sometimes these are done overseas. In recent years, the top-ranking wrestlers are largely foreigners who have come to dominate the sport. Two Mongolian wrestlers are the top-ranked wrestlers with a Bulgarian wrestler working his way up the sumo ladder. The first foreigner to be promoted to the rank of *ozeki*, a step down from the top-ranked *yokozuna*, was a Hawaiian by the name of "Konishiki." He dominated the sport in the 1990s. He was, and still is, huge in size. He could thrust a smaller wrestler out of the ring with little to no effort. Konishiki was never promoted to the top-rank because of a poor performance and that intangible certain-something that is referred to as a "champion's dignity" that the *Sumo* Federation did not feel he possessed. Later, however, another Hawaiian by the name of Chad Rowen (known as Akebono in Japan) did attain the ultimate pinnacle of the *sumo* world by being promoted to *yokozuna*.

Japan certainly wants *sumo* to be accepted internationally, and is working hard to get it recognized as such, but it is causing a bit of a quandary as it is becoming too dominated by foreign wrestlers. By pushing smaller, less powerful Japanese wrestlers to the sidelines, it is creating a sort of cultural conundrum amongst the purists who see *sumo* as a part of its indigenous heritage.

[44] *Transportation System in Japan*

The public transportation system in Japan is a marvel of ingenuity and efficiency. One can get to just about anywhere in the country by public transportation, either by train or bus. The trains are prompt, clean, and modern. If the schedule says the train arrives at 1:42, it does so—on the dot. Buses are equally as exact and adhere to schedules taking into account rush-hour traffic and winter weather conditions.

Japanese people depend upon the public transportation system of trains, subways, and buses to get to and from work every day so it is necessary that everything runs like clockwork and in an orderly fashion. Rarely are trains delayed, but when they are—due to weather, a suicide, or mechanical failure—it throws tens-of-thousands of people off a perfectly timed schedule.

When a delay does occur, train personnel are often at the exit wicket handing out papers to the delayed commuters explaining the delay. Commuters who are made late to work due to an unforeseen delay can show this slip of paper to their supervisors. Especially in Tokyo, people time their commutes down to the minute including the time it takes to walk to and from the stations. So many Tokyoites must travel from such long distances (sometimes up to 2-hours one way) that every minute is savored and cherished.

It is a well-known fact in Japan that fathers often leave the family home before the children are awake in the morning, and they arrive home well after the children have been put to bed. Some fathers rarely see their children during the week and only interact with them on the weekends or public holidays.

I must travel monthly to Tokyo from my home in Hirosaki on business. On these trips, I feel like I am yanked from a serene, carefree life where I am nearly always able to get a seat on a train or bus with no problem, to being jam-packed like a sardine on the Tokyo trains and subways. It is hard to imagine the mass of people in Tokyo coming and going at all times, hustling to and fro, unless you experience it personally. It is amazing the number of people that can be crammed into a finite space.

When the train doors open, people are literally belched out—pouring forth like ants from a mound after it has been disturbed. In the early morning, on certain train routes, special "pushers" are placed strategically on the platform to help get the stragglers squeezed in as the door closes. It certainly makes one appreciate the solitude of a leisurely commute in the comfort of an air-conditioned car, sipping a cup of coffee, while listening to a favorite CD on the short jaunt to work most people enjoy.

For most Japanese, driving to work is not an option. The traffic jams alone would be enough to make a sane person crazy. But the real problem is what to do with the car once you arrive to your workplace? Parking in Japan tends to be quite expensive and space for employee parking is limited (if any exists at all).

As a people, Japanese generally prefer not to have to touch people, especially strangers (hence the custom of bowing instead of shaking hands). So, you can imagine how much personal courage it takes for a Japanese person to muster when commuting during rush-hour, squashed up against perfect strangers for an hour or so commute.

This type of intimacy is unwillingly accepted because it cannot be helped. Having people smashed against you on all sides takes some getting used to for sure; as an American, I generally have a very clear sense of personal space and like to have an arm's length of space between me and other people. This is just not possible in Tokyo during morning rush-hour. Amazingly, though, with the mass of humanity that uses the public transportation system in Japan each day, people are remarkably polite and respectful of other passengers. The exception to this, however, is the minority of men who take advantage of the situation by improperly touching female passengers.

Morning rush hour on Tokyo train

Until recently, women would often stand mortified, frozen with embarrassment, enduring the unwanted advances rather than fighting back. After the train stopped, they would scurry off thoroughly humiliated. Nowadays, women are fighting back by being more vocal and reporting lewd behavior, forcing train personnel to take action against these men. In Japanese, this type of man is called a *chikan* and is finally being dealt with on a regular basis when improper acts do occur.

Newspapers are reporting such occurrences more frequently it seems and the perpetrators are often middle-aged professionals in prominent positions with families. Favorite targets of these types are schoolgirls in their school uniforms. Girls and women today, though, are much more assertive than in the past and are not afraid to single these men out on a crowded train, humiliating them completely.

The problem is so widespread that the Japan Railway Company started a system of "women-only" train cars where women can ride without fear of being molested. These have proven to be quite popular (and appreciated) by Japanese women who must travel during rush-hour. There have been some unscrupulous women, however, who have falsely accused innocent male commuters of untoward behavior which has distracted from the authentic instances of sexual harassment. These women, hoping to get some quick money, do so in hopes that the commuter will pay apology money quickly to avoid the embarrassment of being singled out by such a charge. I read where some men have started to keep both hands on the hand straps in trains to avoid such situations.

All in all, though, considering the millions of people who use public transportation on a daily basis in Tokyo, the instances of bad behavior or problems resulting from being crammed together so tightly, are quite few statistically. This type of system where people are forced to be in a confined area so close that one's face is practically touching another's, works in Japan because people here have learned the fine art of deference.

They have been conditioned since childhood to be polite and unobtrusive to others. This type of arrangement would not work well in most other countries, likely resulting in mass chaos with people pushing and shoving unnecessarily with fights breaking out for no reason. Just one of the many reasons why I love living in Japan.

[45] *Airports and Air Travel in Japan*

Leave it to the Japanese to make traveling internationally and domestically as worry free and as easy as possible. I am always amazed at how effortless it is to travel by air in Japan nowadays. Many services are available to air-travelers that anticipate every imaginable need. For instance, Japan has an extraordinary delivery system that allows travelers to send big suitcases ahead to the airport.

Since most people travel to the airport by train or bus, this makes changing trains and getting to the airport much easier without worrying about bulky luggage that must be lugged up and down the stairways at train stations. For a nominal sum of money, the delivery company will pick the luggage up at your home and deliver it to the terminal of the airport you are traveling from. This service is available all over Japan and they can usually guarantee 24-hour delivery to the airport. The process is reversed when returning, allowing travelers to send their luggage from the airport to their homes. The company I use regularly wraps my suitcase in plastic and gingerly handles it throughout the delivery process. Rarely is any piece of luggage damaged during delivery in Japan. These companies are called *takubin* and will deliver just about anything, anywhere in Japan.

I can order a turkey in Tokyo and have it delivered still frozen to my door in a day. Fragile items are regularly handled with care without as much as a scratch on the box when it is delivered. This care and concern for packages has me spoiled. Recently I sent a ceramic bowl ensconced in bubble-wrap by airmail to the US. I know it was treated properly on this end. However, when it arrived to its destination it was in a million pieces. Naively, I put a "fragile" sticker on it. When I told a friend whose brother is a mail carrier for the US Postal Service about this, she laughed. She said her brother advised her to check a package by throwing it out her front door onto the asphalt. If it does not break, then it is wrapped properly. The huge volume of packages that go through the US Post Office requires that they be chucked from bin to bin before being delivered. A hard lesson learned.

However, I digress, so back to air travel in Japan…since many people do not have cars, and those who do opt not to drive them to the airport, there are a number of private and public transportation options available. Personally, I usually take a "jumbo taxi" from my home to the prefectural airport. It takes about an hour, and is quite reasonable in price. There is also a city bus that goes to the airport several times a day.

Even though Japan is roughly the size of California, it is much more difficult to travel domestically from north to south. Flights from Aomori to Tokyo take an hour; but by highway bus it takes nine hours; by bullet train around five hours; and by overnight sleeper-train about ten hours.

Airline staff preparing to board passengers onto the plane; the woman standing in the waiting area is on call to help locate wayward passengers should they fail to arrive at the gate in a timely manner

The bullet train is not too bad, but where I live I have to change trains at least once to get to Tokyo. Within the next decade, there should be a bullet train from Aomori City, which will be more convenient, but for the time-being I usually fly to save in travel time.

It never fails that when I am waiting for a flight, airline staff are scurrying about trying to find wayward passengers at the largest domestic airport in Japan, Haneda-Tokyo. With walkie-talkie in hand, they are rushing from the security inspection area to the gate yelling out individual passengers' names, trying to alert them that their flight is about to leave. When they locate the passenger, the airline staff people will often help carry the luggage the person has with them to the gate. Bowing and running at the same time.

This would rarely (if ever) happen at a comparably sized airport in most countries. If you are not there when the cabin door closes, you are out of luck. There are no extraordinary efforts made to find confirmed passengers who have not passed through the gateway.

Japanese airline personnel are well-known for their politeness and neatness in appearance. Flight attendants are so well-trained that they flawlessly perform their duties exactly the same way every time. It is refreshing to be treated nicely as well. When they speak to you, they kneel down to be face to face. They use very polite language, as well as gesturing graciously to assist you with the light, headphones, etc. This is quite a departure from US carriers' treatment of passengers where the flight attendants, standing above you—obviously irritated at being disturbed—bark out "chicken or beef" in a nasty tone of voice.

Yes, I am spoiled at the wonderful service Japanese companies offer their customers. US airlines and related industries could certainly learn a thing or two from their Japanese counterparts. Politeness would be a good place to start.

[46] *The Way of Tea*

Green tea is the Japanese beverage of choice in the mornings, when entertaining guests in the afternoon, and when taking a break. It is the only type of traditional tea grown in Japan, and it is served plain without any milk or sugar. For the first time drinker, it may seem bitter, but just like coffee, it grows on you.

When my cousins came to visit, they were so excited to try green tea that on the airplane ride over they asked for it. When the flight attendant served them, they asked her for milk and sugar. I guess she shot them a look of complete horror, announcing incredulously: "It's green tea…not English tea!" They responded that they knew what it was, but still wanted the milk and sugar. Begrudgingly, she gave them what they wanted. I am sure she was surprised, or maybe even shocked, that they would defile green tea with something as crass and vulgar as sugar and milk.

A master performing the tea ceremony

Green tea is much more than a beverage—it is a national pastime, a cultural institution of sorts, that incorporates the aesthetic beauty of nature, the creativeness of art, the ritual of religion, and culminates in a solemn rite of social interaction between the tea master and his/her guests in the "tea ceremony" (*sado*, meaning "the way of tea" in Japanese).

Green tea originally came to Japan via China during the Nara Period (710-794) by Buddhist monks who brought tea seeds back to Japan with them. However, it was not until 1191 that an industry surrounding the cultivation of tea in Japan truly began. It is believed that a monk named "Eisai" planted seeds he brought from China and hence encouraged the widespread cultivation of tea.

Today half of all the tea grown in Japan comes from Shizuoka Prefecture south of Tokyo. When I was a high school exchange student in Tokyo, my host family took me on a short vacation to Atami in eastern Shizuoka on the bullet train. On our trip, we went through "tea country"—the perfectly manicured terraced tea fields were a wondrous sight to see from the window of the speeding train. Rows upon rows of tea plants covered the rolling hills of the mountains throughout the countryside. Women were bent over in broad-rimmed straw hats busily picking the tea leaves.

For visitors to Japan, attending a formal "tea ceremony" is indeed a treat. When my mother first visited Japan, we were invited to partake in a tea ceremony. All of the women in attendance wore beautiful silk *kimono*. The tea ceremony is very formal and highly ritualized. Much care is taken by the host to select just the right combination of bowls and utensils to use, the perfect dry sweet that is eaten with the tea, and what decorations to use in the *tokonoma*, or alcove, located in the tea room.

Guests approach experiencing the tea ceremony with a sense of reverence and respect for the ritual itself, but also toward the host who has made painstaking preparations, taking into account the season to match aesthetically colors, textures and flavors to make the ceremony a once in a lifetime event. In fact, each time the tea ceremony is performed, it is regarded as a singular occurrence or event that cannot be repeated exactly—the same season, the same guests, the same sweets, the same atmosphere. That moment in time can only happen once and can never be exactly replicated.

The tea ceremony requires that guests sit *seiza* (sitting on one's knees). For Japanese, this is not a problem as they are able to sit for endless periods in this position. Not so for people who are not used to sitting like this for long periods of time. My mother, after about twenty minutes, finally leaned over and told me she could not feel her legs. An astute guest sensed my mother's discomfort and retrieved for her a small stool that allowed her to sit in the proper position, but shifted the weight from her legs to the stool. This made my mother very happy and allowed her to enjoy the tea ceremony more fully.

Actually, foreign visitors are given much leeway in the etiquette department when it comes to the tea ceremony. It is such a foreign concept to anything that we experience, that most Japanese hosts forgive most indiscretions regarding the proper procedure and ritual associated with the tea ceremony and accommodate first-time visitors accordingly.

Upon arrival, guests for the tea ceremony are ushered into a waiting area where they are able to sample the hot water used in the ceremony. Often times, the guests will select from among them the "main guest" who will act as leader of the group. This is usually an esteemed person who is a teacher or elder of the others.

Once the host acknowledges them, they are led by the main guest to the tea garden where they may sit for a few moments on benches to enjoy the natural beauty of the meticulously kept garden. If available, the guests will ceremoniously wash their hands in a *tsukubai* or stone basin. This is largely symbolic, representing that the guests cleanse themselves of any worldly concerns before entering the actual tea house. The order that the guests rinse their hands is the order that they will be served throughout the entire tea ceremony.

A true tea house requires that the guests crawl through a small sliding door called a *nijiriguchi*. This requires that the guests crouch low on their knees to enter the room. I was told this symbolizes the idea that all are considered equal and no one person has status or prestige over another while in the confines of the tea room. Each guest upon entering the tea room reverently admires the scroll hanging in the alcove (selected for the occasion and the season). They then seat themselves around the edge of the room in the order they decided earlier during the cleansing in the garden.

The host then prepares the tea in a very systematic and practiced manner that represents centuries of tradition. The tea is powdered and mixed with hot water from an iron teapot using a wooden ladle. The host then whips the tea with a traditional whisk made from bamboo. The main guest is served the first bowl of tea by bowing to the host before picking the bowl up and cupping it in both hands. The bowl is turned three times before taking the first sip.

Many tea masters have studied and honed their ability for decades. My university has a tea ceremony club, and many of the students who belong have studied it since they were in elementary or junior high school. It is certainly a very representative part of Japanese culture, and any visitor to Japan, if given the opportunity, should experience this traditional art form.

Just don't ask for milk and sugar for your tea.

[47] *Voting and the Election System in Japan*

With America's most recent presidential election having taken place in November 2008, I thought it appropriate to comment about the Japanese system of elections. Often people overseas ask if I am allowed to vote in Japan and if I take the time to vote in the US.

I am not a Japanese citizen, so I do not have the right to vote in Japan. I do have "permanent residency" which means I have permission to live here indefinitely. When I first came to Japan, I was on a "professor's visa" which had to be renewed every three years. My status as "permanent resident" allows me to come and go, to and from Japan as I wish without worrying about a visa. However, this does not mean that I have Japanese citizenship, so therefore I cannot vote. I carry a US passport and I am still American—I just happen to live in Japan and have done so for over 20 years. I have no intention of immigrating to Japan and becoming, in essence, "Japanese."

Many people back home, not understanding clearly immigration and permanent resident issues, ask me if I have given up my US citizenship because of the length of time I have lived in Japan. This is not something I have ever entertained. I am happy with my nationality; I just like living and working in Japan. I do see myself after retirement dividing my time between the two countries—one foot in Japan and the other in the United States. However, there are a growing number of expatriates living in Japan who do, in fact, opt to take Japanese citizenship, hence becoming Japanese.

I do vote by absentee ballot in US elections. The Election Board in the city that I maintain residence in the US does a magnificent job in making sure I get my ballot in enough time to get it back before the election takes place. In each election cycle, I always vote early so my ballot is snuggly stored at the courthouse awaiting the general election.

I have never missed voting in a national election, and I honestly cannot remember missing a local election. I feel strongly that in a democracy it is each citizen's obligation to cast a vote in order to be heard. Hence, if I do not like how politicians are running things, I feel I have every right to voice my displeasure because by voting I have a stake in the process and outcome.

Just like in many democracies, Japan normally has a low voter turnout. That is why the 2008 US Presidential Election was so exciting because so many first-time voters turned out to have their voices heard. In past elections, it seems that people had become complacent and figured that one vote could not make that much of a difference and therefore many chose not to be heard. As we have seen in the US, indeed every vote does count and can make a huge difference in an outcome.

The national election system in Japan has been in place since the late 1890s. Of course, like most countries around the world, including the US, it limited voting to a narrow portion of the entire population. At that time, only adult males who paid annual taxes in a predetermined amount could vote. In the 1920s, the right to vote was expanded to all males 25 years-of-age or older. Shortly after World War II, universal suffrage was adopted allowing all the right to vote, including women. The current system in Japan has been in place since 1950, a combination of prewar practice and revised postwar additions. Today, all Japanese citizens the age of 20 or older have the right to vote; there is a three month residency requirement if voting in local elections.

The Japanese nationally elected body, collectively, is called the "Diet." It is the highest authority of state power and is charged with the duty of making laws for Japan. The Diet consists of two chambers: the House of Representatives (lower house) and the House of Councilors (upper house). All members of the Diet are elected through a popular vote by Japanese citizens. Unlike in the US where the President is elected directly by the people, the Prime Minister of Japan is a member of the ruling party and is selected by majority vote in each House of the Diet. After this takes place, the selected Prime Minister is then officially appointed to the position by the emperor.

The Liberal Democratic Party (LDP) has consistently maintained control for nearly the entire period of time since it was created in 1955. Since I have lived in Japan, a number of scandals have plagued the LDP causing a revolving door effect with Prime Ministers resigning and new ones being instated. A number of years ago, Japanese voters voted in members of an opposition party and the control changed briefly. That was quite remarkable, but short-lived, though, and since that one brief interruption the LDP has been the primary ruling party in Japan.

A recent Prime Minister, Koizumi, lasted the longest in my memory. Many people might be familiar with him because of his funky hairstyle and his obsession with Elvis Presley. On an official visit to the US, President George W. Bush took him to Graceland where Mr. Koizumi shook his hips Elvis-style and serenaded Pricilla and Lisa Marie Presley with a not-so-good rendition of "Love me Tender." It made headlines here, as well as all over the world.

The Prime Minister after Koizumi—Shintaro Abe—had a very short run in the top spot. Of course, the missile situation with North Korea regarding its saber rattling, as well as the abduction issue involving the kidnapping of Japanese nationals decades ago who were forced to live and teach Japanese to North Korean agents, gave him a "baptism by fire" in the finer points of international diplomacy. He was not able to stand the heat, however, and was forced to resign.

In one area, however, Abe gained points with women voters in that he seemed to have a genuine marriage and equal partnership with his wife, even taking her on an official trip to China where he publicly held her hand—which made more headlines than the issues discussed at the meeting.

Traditionally, wives of prime ministers are rarely seen, and when they are, they usually walk several steps behind their husbands. For Japanese people, seeing former Prime Minister Abe walk hand-in-hand with his wife was surprising, and a definite departure from the norm.

Elections in Japan are strictly regulated. The candidates can only campaign for a fixed amount of time, posting small headshot posters in designated areas, and campaign funding is but a mere fraction in Japan of what it is in an American congressional race. Actually, it seems obscene (with so much poverty in the United States and in the world) at how much money is funneled into electing a US President, Senator or Congressman. Japanese candidates' election campaigns are quite simple, in comparison, and certainly less expensive. Japanese election hopefuls usually ride around in minivans waving at passersby. Often they have the van filled with young women, dressed in identical clothing, waving along with them.

This seems quite sexist to me. The women are basically there to smile and look pretty…which has nothing to do with the candidate's ability to be a good representative. No matter. This is the routine that all Japanese politicians follow when trying to get elected…and it obviously works because it is the common and preferred way Japanese politicians choose to garner the public's votes.

The most annoying part about Japanese elections for me is the noise pollution they generate. The minivans are equipped with huge sound systems that have someone constantly blurting out the candidate's name. When two opposing minivans happen upon the same street, the noise is deafening.

Although the political system in Japan is largely based on the British model, it is not nearly as nasty as US and British elections. Constituents in Japan are not bombarded with smear campaigns by candidates against their opponents. Comparatively speaking, I much prefer the Japanese election cycle. It is much shorter and definitely cheaper. The discomfort of a couple weeks of candidates in Japan screaming their name over and over on a loud speaker is much more tolerable than the US custom of candidates inundating everyone's TVs for a year or more with mean-spirited and hostile mud-slinging—and spending hundreds of millions of dollars in the process. What a waste.

[48] *Pop-Concerts not only for Teenagers*

As a teenager, I was never that keen about attending "rock" concerts. In college, I only went to a couple. I was never crazy about any one group, musician, or singer that compelled me to be a "fan." However, since living in Japan I have gone to a number of concerts. A few years ago, I traveled to Tokyo with a gaggle of friends who truly are "fans" to attend a "pop" concert of a boy band that has been around for over two decades. They were in their early teens when they first performed as a group. The group is called "SMAP" and it is made up of five guys who have parlayed their teenage dream of pop-stardom into a huge multi-faceted—almost cult-like—mega-industry.

Too often, teeny-bopper groups quickly get classified into the "one-hit-wonder" category because after their initial burst of stardom, they fade into oblivion, never to be heard from again. Not these guys. They have maintained their "hotness" throughout the years, progressively expanding their fan base with each new generation that comes into contact with their music. Rarely can one pick up a magazine or turn a channel on television and not see at least one, if not all, of these guys. They are featured in commercials, act in TV dramas, host TV shows, appear in movies, write books, and, of course, sell a lot of music CDs and DVDs.

I was a bit worried, at first, when my friend called to ask if I would go with her. I did not want us to be lost in a crowd of teenagers, the only middle-aged people in the audience—two old codgers amidst a sea of young kids screaming their heads off. As it turned out, we were just two early-middle-aged-people among tens-of-thousands of 30-50 year-old women screaming their heads off. Of course, there were young children there, as well, and teenagers, university students, young adults, but overwhelmingly, the crowd consisted of older women. There were even elderly people teetering around the venue with canes in hand.

A sampling of some of the goods available to diehard fans for the group SMAP

My friend is a big fan of this group and she came to the concert very prepared. I was strictly instructed that I had to wear a red shirt and hat. Each of us was color coordinated in an "official" SMAP color that represented one of the five group members. She wore pink; another person in our group wore green; and another blue. It seems that the hardcore fans of this group know this fact. I was clueless and felt a bit silly, but once I arrived, I realized how serious these fans were about supporting their favorite group member by wearing the color associated with him.

Since the color of a person's clothing signals which group member you like the best, for those who cannot decide on just one member will mix the colors, rooting for their "favorites." The particular performer for whom I was dressed in red was Takuya Kimura, better known by his legions of fans as "Kimitaku" (a combination of his last and first names).

Before the concert, we had to arrive early in order to stand in line to view and buy the many "goods" associated with the group. My friend had a "wish" list from friends who were not lucky enough to get one of the more than 50,000 tickets sold for that particular show. The official SMAP products include anything from washcloths and towels to flashlights and oversized hand fans that feature each member's face prominently, but separately. Which means…many of these women opted to buy all five in order to have a complete set. Lighted flashlights were also sold, and I think every person in the arena had one. You do the math. Somebody made a whole lot of money on this concert tour.

During the actual concert, each song seemed to have its own particular hand movements that went along with the lyrics. Seemingly everyone knew this but me; I tried to keep up the best I could, mimicking everyone else around me. It was a spectacle to behold—50,000 screaming fans moving their fans and lights in unison throughout the entire 3 ½ hour concert. The boys do know how to put on a show. Actually, they are much better performers than they are singers, in my opinion. It is the whole package, though, that makes them so popular, causing normally demure and reserved Japanese women to scream like banshees.

The show featured pyrotechnics, loud booms, smoke, and a jungle-themed stage setting with a waterfall. Two cranes lifted the members up into the ethers of the arena so those poor souls stuck in the hinterlands could have a closer look at their favorite group members. Fortunately, our seats were on the main floor, next to the side stage, which gave us a very close look at the members. This thrilled my friend to pieces. At one point, she held up a sign that said "thank you" and one of the members acknowledged her with a thumb's up gesture. I thought she was going to faint.

Initially, the group entered the arena from the ceiling, sliding down steel cables to the floor. For the finale, they rode around the entire stadium floor in cherry picker-like contraptions that hoisted them up and down to make eye contact with as many people as they could. During their costume changes, the audience was treated to a mini-movie in 3-D. Each audience member had a set of 3-D glasses in which to view the program. As thrilling as the concert was, though, what really impressed me was the politeness of the fans. Unlike American concerts where people push and shove trying to get closer to the stage, each fan at the SMAP concert stayed in his/her seat, never encroaching upon another's space.

Although there were security guards and staff standing around everywhere, they had nothing to do, really, because no one tried to run onto the stage, jump the barrier or do anything that was not permitted. I witnessed not one instance of tom-foolery being perpetrated by a dumb fan. Everyone just enjoyed the concert from the seat that was assigned to them.

After the concert finished, with everyone still whipped up into a crazed fervor, the stadium lights came on and an announcer politely asked everyone to stay seated until he released the section they were sitting in. From the top to the bottom, 50,000 people filed out quietly and orderly. This was the most amazing part for me—tens of thousands of people waiting diligently as each section was released, then standing and calmly exiting the arena. There was no pushing, shoving, or jostling of any sort.

I cannot imagine the reaction of a crowd at an American event with the same number of people in attendance being asked to stay seated until told they could leave. People would be incensed that they could not leave immediately. In contrast, Japanese people do not usually have that overpowering urge to get out as quickly as possible in these types of situations. For instance, after a film finishes in a theater, Japanese people nearly all stay seated until the very last credit rolls up the screen and the house lights come on.

In the US, a film is barely finished when people start rustling about, crawling over other people, trying to exit the theater as quickly as possible. It is a "beat the crowd" mentality—even if it means standing in line to get out the door or sitting in your car waiting for traffic to clear.

I have now become so accustomed to sitting in a theater until all the credits have finished that when I go to a movie in the US, family and friends think it strange to sit and read every credit that passes by.

Sometimes I am left sitting alone in the theater…which is fine by me.

[49] *Japanese Homes—Understated Elegance and Simplicity*

Since Japan is geographically positioned in such a way that it experiences every extreme in weather, houses are designed to take this into account. For instance, with the exception of the northernmost island of Hokkaido, Japan goes through a rather heavy rainy season called *tsuyu* every year. This is why Japan is so lush and green with thick vegetation. As expected, the summer's sweltering heat and high humidity make it necessary for houses to be able to breathe. This is why, since ancient times, Japanese architecture has focused on how to protect homes from mold and mildew.

A traditional Japanese home with *tatami* and *fusuma*

Traditionally, homes have always been made light and flexible to allow air to move through easily. Even in the snow country where I reside, houses are not as tight and sealed as they would be the northern areas in other parts of the world. In addition, since Japan suffers from frequent and powerful earthquakes, a flexible structure is more able to sustain a robust jolt. This is why Japan's beautiful medieval castles were all made of wood and not stone. The wood would bend and sway during an earthquake; where as a brick or stone structure would most likely topple over. Unfortunately, though, the wood structures did not hold up so well to fire and the majority of Japanese castles throughout the centuries fell victim to blazes—either intentionally set by an enemy faction or by freak lightning strikes.

Fire, and the fear of fire, always occupies Japanese people's minds. Because houses are built of wood and are so close together, coupled with the fact that many are built on narrow streets in neighborhoods off main thoroughfares, make it difficult for big fire engines to enter in an emergency. A raging fire can quickly become widespread burning a number of homes in an area. In the old days, each evening, a man would walk the streets with two pieces of wood that he clanged together to remind people to put out their stove fires before bedtime. In some places, this custom still exists. I remember hearing it in a small village in southern Japan a number of years ago.

In addition to homes being made primarily of wood in Japan, the floors are generally raised to add space between the structure and damp ground. Today, newer homes are sometimes being built on cement slabs which are a departure from traditional methods. These often are equipped with "floor heating" for the winter and are somehow designed to resist potential mold issues that are always a concern for homeowners here. A traditional Japanese home has few stationary walls with hinged doors. Instead, homes are built with moveable walls that act as room dividers called *fusuma*. Also, paper (*shoji*) sliding doors between rooms, and paper window coverings to outside windows, allow air and light to pass through; these offer the appearance of being substantial and private, but are made of rice paper and are actually very thin. Japanese people can find privacy in their own personal space without being shut up in a walled room with a hinged door. Even though *shoji* doors are primarily made of paper, people can still feel they have privacy even with family members on the other side chatting away.

Although fragile, and sometimes a nuisance for families with small children because little fingers find it amusing to poke holes in the paper squares, this type of covering is quite versatile and elegant in appearance. Japanese homes, because of the moveable doors that can be opened or closed with ease, allow rooms to be used for a variety of purposes. By day, they can be used for entertaining guests during afternoon tea, using a low table in the center of the room surrounded by cushions called *zabuton*. At night, the table can be pushed to the side of the room and be transformed into a bedroom. A closet located on half of a wall (called an *o-shire*) stores the bedding during the day; the other half of the wall next to the closet usually features an alcove called a *tokunoma*.

The *tokunoma* normally has a traditional scroll hanging in it with some type of art piece or flower arrangement displayed on the floor of the niche. The flooring in this room is *tatami* (straw mats) and the walls are normally made of a traditional earthen material that is green in color. Japanese homes that are Western in design will usually have at least one traditional Japanese *tatami* room. Because of the upkeep, though, some new homes lay flooring which is longer lasting and less trouble to clean, foregoing *tatami* all together.

Of course, in the big cities, like Tokyo, owning a home with a yard is so expensive that many families rent apartments or purchase condominiums in high-rises. A typical-style apartment is usually a 2LDK (two bedrooms with a combined living/dining/kitchen area). Although small by Western standards, a family of four in Japan can occupy this type of apartment with no problem. Given a choice, however, Japanese families prefer to have their own home. The dream of owning one's own home in Japan is as strong as it is in other countries. Recently, more and more Japanese have been able to realize this dream, a trend referred to as "My Home"—securing a bank loan, buying land, and building a modest home for one's family.

[50] *Travel Hints—Arriving and Finding a Hotel in Tokyo*

I remember arriving in Tokyo on my first trip outside the USA as a 17-year-old exchange student and just being absolutely awestruck at everything. The whole caboodle was so foreign, naturally, but to this small-town kid from Indiana, it went beyond that. I was embarking upon an adventure of a lifetime which would eventually have a great influence upon my future life and career. Of course, I did not know that then. At that moment, all I could think about was, "Wow! I'm in Japan."

Adding to the excitement was the fact that the 70s disco group "Peaches and Herb" were on our plane and happened to be in the immigration line with us. Of course, we all got autographs and snapped rolls of film, commemorating this brush with fame.

I was reminded of this experience when an acquaintance of my family wrote to ask about what places I recommend visiting while in Japan. This was her first trip abroad, and definitely, she planned to visit Japan's equivalent of the "Big Apple." She wanted some inside information on how to get around, where to stay, eat, tour, and shop in Tokyo.

First and foremost, doing Japan on your own is admirable, but can be quite daunting for the first time visitor. Of course, Japan today is a far cry from 1979 when I came the first time, but it can still give a first-time visitor a run for his/her money. Immediately upon arriving at Tokyo's Narita Airport, travelers are met with a cacophony of sights and sounds that sometimes leave them speechless. The immense size and the volume of people coming and going in all directions in the terminal can be jarring to the uninitiated.

Today, it is a very modern and international airport with signs in English to help guide you. When I first came to Japan, there were no Romanized or English signs except for the sign guiding travelers to immigration. A green and black lighted sign had the word "ALIEN" in huge letters. It seemed so odd to me that I was compelled to snap a photo of it. Fortunately, those signs have been replaced with more tasteful ones that do not make visitors feel so unwelcome or like a creature from outer space. In fact, since that time, Japan has done remarkably well in incorporating easy to understand directions and signs for visitors with no command of the Japanese language.

From the airport to downtown Tokyo is quite a jaunt. I do not recommend jumping into a taxi for the nearly two-hour trip unless you have the equivalent of $250 in yen burning a hole in your pocket. Besides, if time is a factor, the express train from the airport to Tokyo Station is much faster anyway because one never knows what kind of traffic is waiting on the expressway between the airport and central Tokyo. For a reasonable fare, it is easy to hop on the "Narita Express" train that takes you to the heart of Tokyo. There are several other train options, which are cheaper, but some are local trains that have many stops and others end at stations that are not as convenient. The trains are clean, comfortable and efficient, making the trip quite enjoyable and hassle free. There is also a limousine bus service from the airport to a variety of destinations in and around Tokyo, but one has to take into account that pesky traffic that can sometimes make the normally 90 minute trip into one that takes several hours.

I highly recommend arranging hotel accommodations before arriving in Tokyo. There are literally thousands of hotels—in all price ranges—but getting a room on demand can be a bit sticky if it is during high season or coincidentally corresponds with a big event taking place in Tokyo. For the high-end visitor who is not on a budget, there are exceptional hotels that can make a person feel like royalty… but you need a princely purse to pay for it. The Park Hyatt was the hotel featured in the film *Lost in Translation* and has one of the best reputations for service and amenities.

For the discriminating, but cash-conscious traveler, one can find suitable accommodations at reasonable rates (for Tokyo) costing $60-$100 per person per night. In Japan, Western-style and traditional-style hotels charge per person and not per room. So, if a couple wants to reserve a room, they would pay a "twin-rate" and usually be given a room with two twin beds. Many budget hotels in Japan exclusively have either single rooms or twin rooms. Hotels that cater to foreign guests will sometimes have double or queen-sized beds, but the charge is still per person and not per room.

I think the average Japanese couple must prefer separate beds, because few budget hotels offer a double bed (let alone a queen or king-sized bed). When my mother and step-father came to visit, a friend reserved their hotel for them in Tokyo. He assumed, because of their age, they would want to have twin beds (like Japanese married couples). It surprised them to see two twin beds, instead of two double or queen-sized beds, which is more standard in the United States and what they expected.

I have several hotels that I routinely use when on business in Tokyo. These fall into the category of "business hotel" which means the rooms are small, compact, but clean. These hotels, as the name suggests, cater to businesspeople that basically need a comfortable and convenient place to sleep without the frills of more higher-priced hotels (bellhops, room-service, valet service, etc).

The traditional Japanese inn, or *ryokan*, is a nice choice for visitors who want to experience traditional Japan. The prices tend to be as expensive, or more so, as Western-style hotels, but a Japanese breakfast is often included in the price which usually consists of rice, *miso* soup, fish and *daikon* (radish) or some other vegetable. The rooms are covered with *tatami* mats, so no shoes are permitted inside; and guests sleep on *futon* on the floor. These rooms usually have a low table with cushions, but often no chairs are provided. Sometimes, only a toilet is a part of the room, with guests using a traditional Japanese-style communal bath for bathing. Most *ryokan* in Tokyo, however, tend to offer both—a full bath in each room and the option of bathing in a communal bath on the main floor. Guests are given cotton *yukatta* (robe) and slippers to use while at the hotel.

[51] *Travel Hints—Touring Tokyo and Finding Restaurants*

Although I am not a big fan of guided "group" tours, I highly recommend taking a bus tour of Tokyo for the first-time visitor who wants to pack as much as possible into a finite amount of time. The reason is that unless you have lots of time, and are not afraid of getting terribly lost, it is just easier and in the end, more enjoyable to be driven around to all the major sites.

After years of traveling back and forth to Tokyo for business and pleasure, I have learned to maneuver around this sprawling city with a certain degree of confidence and success. However, it still takes a lot time to get from point A to point B. Finding the station, catching the right train, changing trains, switching to the subway network, climbing stairs, finding the correct exit, hiking to the site you want to see, then doing it all in reverse...and again to go to the next place...well...you get the picture.

Touring Tokyo on a guided bus tour is an easy way for tourists to not only see the sites but also to learn about the history of the places they visit

The Japanese have certainly perfected the art of doing "bus tours" by making them not only comfortable and convenient, but also quite informative. The full-service bus drops the group off at the exact place of interest, with an English speaking guide, and picks the group up afterward to go to the next site. The bus route is meticulously laid out to make it time effective, hitting the major points of interest in a very organized and efficient manner. When my cousins came to visit, we signed up for a half-day tour that took us to all the major places of historic and cultural interest in Tokyo. I loved it because it took the pressure off me to be host, tour guide, and Japan-expert. It made the best use of our limited amount of time, while being very informative and interesting.

No city on earth has as many restaurants and bars as Tokyo. One can find any type of food from Ethiopian to Mongolian to South American…and anything and everything in between. For the visitor who wants to experience the real Japan, a traditional *sushi* bar would be a good choice because you cannot get fresher fish anywhere else. In fact, sometimes the fish is still moving when the master chef sets the plate down in front of you. Not for the fainthearted, for sure.

A window display of the various foods offered in the restaurant…all plastic facsimiles

If seafood or fish is not your cup of tea, there are other wonderfully delicious delicacies that are quite agreeable to the Western palate. *Yakitori* (skewered chicken), *tonkatsu* (breaded pork tenderloin), or *tempura* are some examples. For meat lovers, a visit to a typical *yakiniku* restaurant would be a treat. These restaurants are actually Korean in origin, but are prevalent and abundant all over Japan. In the center of the table is a *hibachi* grill where the meat is cooked. The uncooked meat is brought to the table, and each person grills the meat to his/her liking. Side orders of vegetables can be ordered to be grilled alongside the meat, and of course, white sticky rice is eaten, along with mugs of beer to wash it all down.

Nightlife in Tokyo is world-renowned, especially the area called "Roppongi." This part of Tokyo seems to be a magnet for foreign tourists wanting to barhop and dance the night away. It is a bit too seedy for my tastes, but it is worth a gander to those who want to see what Tokyo's nightlife has to offer. In recent years this area has tried to cleanup its image by creating tony areas for dining and shopping, but at night can still be a bit dicey.

Even though Tokyo is one of the largest cities in the world, it is actually quite safe, especially for tourists. It is very rare for tourists to be taken advantage of by unscrupulous people in Japan. Taxi drivers are well-known for their honesty, unlike other big cities where you have to be on your guard in order not to be taken for a ride. Also, Japanese taxis are neat, clean and always in good mechanical condition.

One area that does have a reputation for being a tad bit dangerous, especially at night, is "Kabuki-cho." It is here that much of the sex-related industry is located, with Asian and Japanese gangs being visibly present. In the old days, many of the big movie theaters were in this area, making it necessary to venture there. Today, bigger, more modern, and much more elegant theaters dot the city, making it less likely to have to go to this part of town.

[52] *Travel Hints—Sightseeing and Shopping in Tokyo*

One aspect of Japan that I am regularly impressed with is how elegant and courteous department store clerks are when serving the store's customers. Few countries undertake department stores as well as Japan. Sleek, modern, trendy, and swanky are a few words to describe shopping in one of these state-of-the-art emporiums. If one is lucky enough to arrive as the doors open in the morning, the first customers of the day are treated to lines of perfectly dressed employees in neatly pressed uniforms and suits greeting shoppers with deep, respectful bows. It is this type of detail that make Japanese department stores stand out from the ordinary. Also, women clerks are strictly trained in how to speak and how to gesture toward customers, incorporating only the politest of language while using the most graceful of hand movements.

A department store employee greeting the first customers of the day

The first-time visitor to Tokyo would do well to see the Tokyo Tower. Not because as a structure it is so unique (the Eiffel Tower of Paris is much more quaint), but because it offers a bird's-eye-view of how endlessly expansive Tokyo appears to be. Tokyo Tower's bright red and white steel frame is tacky at best, but on a clear day one can catch a majestic glimpse of Mount Fuji, along with all the skyscrapers and buildings that are packed together in every direction.

Time permitting…a few days in Japan's ancient capital, Kyoto, is a trip worth taking. Kyoto offers so much to the visitor who wants to experience traditional Japan; ancient temples, shrines, pagodas, and near there, Himeji castle that is an original structure that was spared destruction by early reformists and the odd lightning strike.

I would be remiss if I did not promote my lovely city—Hirosaki, Aomori Prefecture. Albeit smaller in scale than Kyoto, Hirosaki offers many of the same traditional structures (including an original castle guardhouse), but in a setting that is more serene and less crowded. It is called the "little Kyoto of the north." Only occasionally do I receive visitors from home who want to see a part of Japan that few ever get a chance to experience. It is quite a trek to get here, though, which precludes visitors from just dropping by. A real effort and advance planning is needed to come to the hinterlands of Honshu island.

However, if Tokyo is the only place on your itinerary, the determined tourist can indeed experience traditional Japan there, as well. I highly recommend a visit to "Meiji Shrine." Strolling through its meticulously kept grounds makes one forget that outside the gates is the hustle bustle of downtown Tokyo. If you are lucky, a newlywed couple in *kimono* may be getting a formal wedding photo taken with the shrine as a backdrop. Another *Shinto* shrine that is fun to see is "Asakusa Shrine." Slowly making your way to the shrine down the narrow street is the fun part. Lining each side of the street are traditional stalls and shops hawking everything Japanese from food to trinkets.

The Imperial Palace is interesting to see because of its extensive gardens and grounds. Of course, tourists do not get anywhere near the imperial family's quarters, but visitors are shown enough to get an idea of what life must be like behind the imposing stone walls and moats. There are some really great places to get snapshots with buildings and palace walls as background.

The "Ginza" is internationally notorious for having some of the priciest real estate in the world. After World War II, this area of Tokyo quickly became the center of high fashion and high prices. If you are in the market for a strand of cultured pearls, this is the place to go. Mikimoto's flagship store is located in the heart of the Ginza.

The areas of "Shibuya" and "Harajuku" are where the young and fashionable hang out. It is fun just to stand on a corner for several minutes to "people watch" because any and every type of fashion trend can be seen in these two areas. It offers a glimpse into "what's hot and what's not" in the Tokyo fashion world. Japanese young people take fashion and accessorizing quite seriously; if it is in style, it will be seen here.

Outside Shibuya Station is a crosswalk that is worth experiencing once. When the light turns green for pedestrians, literally thousands of people crisscross the wide avenue in every direction making a newcomer dizzy trying to take it all in, while at the same time, trying to avoid getting trampled.

In Harajuku, a narrow alleyway running a number of blocks called "Takeshita Dori" is heaven on earth for young people trying to find the latest apparel, shoes, bags, or other fashion-related goods. A word of warning: It is usually wall to wall people, so you must charge forward aggressively to make your way, like salmon swimming upstream. At the other end of Takeshita Dori, it is a short walk to the Champs-

Elysées of Tokyo—Omotesando. This tree lined boulevard caters to the well-heeled and trendiest of shoppers. Where the Ginza attracts older and wealthy shoppers, Omotesando is geared toward the mid-twenties to mid-forties business and career minded crowd. A very high-end and elegant shopping plaza which opened there is called "Omotesando Hills." It is enjoyable to stroll in its uniquely designed mall that goes deep underground. The actual physical space is quite small in comparison to malls in other countries, but the architects and designers created an illusion of having vast space in an area that is actually quite narrow.

I recommend the "Oriental Bazaar" on this same boulevard for souvenir shopping. One can find antiques, new or used *kimono*, as well as ceramics, books, and just about anything Japanese in this store. However, instead of carrying your Japanese baubles and mementos throughout the rest of your trip, you can hold off and visit a branch of the Oriental Bazaar at Narita Airport on your way home. Although it is a much more scaled down version of the main store, there are plenty of souvenirs to choose from and for the same price. There is no mark-up because it is at the airport.

The truly budget-conscious traveler would do well to visit a Japanese version of a "dollar" store called "100 Yen Shop." These stores are everywhere and the variety of merchandise is unbelievable. It is very easy to find Japanese-type souvenirs for family and friends back home. It can be your secret that the gift cost less than a US dollar—one of the few bargains in Japan.

Doing Japan on a shoestring budget is not easy. It is best to come with fistfuls of money because it is not cheap. A budget traveler can have an enjoyable stay, but most visitors, after the initial sticker-shock, do eventually succumb to spending more than they intended, no matter how frugal they try to be. It's Japan, after all.

[53] *Much Gained, More to Learn from Experiencing Foreign Cultures*

A reader of my blog once wrote to ask where besides Japan I have traveled to, and where is my favorite place of all the destinations I have visited. That is such a difficult question to answer. I have been blessed over the years to have been afforded many opportunities to live in different parts of the world and to travel to just about every continent, with the exception of Antarctica.

As I was growing up in Shelbyville, Indiana—very middle America—I never imagined in my wildest dreams the type of life I would eventually lead. I always had a fascination with foreign languages and cultures and this allure became even stronger once I first traveled to Japan as a summer exchange student while a junior in high school.

That first exposure of living in a foreign culture as a teenager has led me to live in Europe, Central America, and Asia. As a university student, I spent my junior year abroad in Madrid, Spain. As a post-graduate student, I lived in San Jose, Costa Rica as a Rotary Scholar.

With that said, I cannot pinpoint one particular place that I would say is my favorite, except to say that each and every place I have had the great fortune to explore offers a unique and different cross-cultural experience. I can, however, list a few of the high points…and even some low points of my travels.

A definite highlight was when I went on an elephant back safari in the foothills of the Himalayas in Thailand. This experience, along with seeing all of the cultural and historic places, stands out in my mind. I also enjoyed seeing the terraced rice paddies of Bali, Indonesia, along with the culture and traditions of this fascinating tropical island.

Doing the "hokey-pokey" on the Great Wall of China with a group of school kids was another highlight, as well as seeing the mass of clay soldiers unearthed in an imperial tomb in Xian, China. Traveling through China had its challenges, but was well worth it to experience such a diverse and ancient culture.

When I lived in Spain, I traveled all over the Iberian Peninsula, even skiing in Andorra (the principality between Spain and France in the Pyrenees), visiting Portugal several times, and sunbathing in the Spanish Canary Islands off the coast of Africa (as well as traveling to a number of other European countries).

Living in Japan allows me to visit easily a number of countries around Asia and the surrounding area. I have visited Korea, Indonesia, Singapore, Hong Kong, Malaysia, Las Marianas (Saipan and Guam), Australia and of course, Thailand and China. Within Japan, I have made an effort to travel to all regions of the archipelago, from north to south, including Okinawa.

Balinese women in Indonesia with food offerings en route to a Hindu festival

On the downside, being chased by a raging bull on a mountainside in Spain would be a low point. I learned not to take shortcuts through fenced fields. My friends and I ran screaming like girls across the open field, making it over the fence just in time. Being 22-years-old had its advantages, as I probably would not be so quick on my feet today. It does make a good story to tell at cocktail parties, though. Needless to say, I never participated in the running of the bulls in Pamplona after this harrowing experience. I had no desire to repeat that sensation after my own impromptu version of this famous Spanish festival. Also, I figured I should not press my luck.

As well, I have been chased by a pack of wild monkeys in Bali, and came face-to-face with a wild-boar on a jungle trek in Costa Rica. I will not even mention the snakes I have encountered in my adventures. Also, I was pick pocketed in Costa Rica, scammed by a taxi con-artist in Bogotá, Colombia, and had a knife pulled on me in Madrid in an attempted robbery. Thankfully I was not injured in any of these instances, but these experiences made me a much better traveler and made me much more aware of my surroundings. After visiting Noriega's Panama, I was stopped at the border and had "bonificado" stamped in my passport (meaning I had gone over the allowable limit of "goods") which prohibited me from returning to Panama for six months because I had purchased twelve pairs of shoes. The border patrol thought I was smuggling shoes to resell in Costa Rica, when in fact they were all for my personal use. I like shoes, what can I say?

A similar thing happened when I was returning to Costa Rica from Colombia; I had to submit to a full body search because I had ten wool sweaters in my luggage. I purchased them for my family as gifts. Unbeknownst to me, drug runners sometimes used the wool in sweaters to hide drugs. An embarrassing experience, indeed, but at least my family got sweaters for Christmas that year.

All in all, though, traveling abroad has allowed me to meet some very interesting and colorful people. It has also humbled me greatly by showing me just how much I do not know about our great big world and how much I still need to learn. In actuality, I have only scratched the surface.

About the Author

Todd Jay Leonard lives, writes, and teaches in Japan where he is a university professor. He has published extensively in academic journals, magazines and newspapers on cross-cultural, historical, and Teaching English as a Foreign Language (TEFL) themes. His publications include *Crossing Cultures: America and Japan* (Kenkyusha, 1992); *Extra! Extra! Read All About It!* (Kinseido, 1994); *Team-Teaching Together: A Bilingual Resource Handbook for JTEs and AETs* (Taishukan, 1994); *Talk, Talk: American-Style* (Macmillan Languagehouse, 1996); *Words to Write By: Developing Writing Skills through Quotations* (Macmillan Languagehouse, 1997); *The Better Half: Exploring the Changing Roles of Men and Women with Current Newspaper Articles* (Macmillan Languagehouse, 1997); *East Meets West: An American in Japan* (Kenkyusha, 1998); *East Meets West: Problems and Solutions—Understanding Misunderstandings between JTEs and ALTs* (Taishukan, 1999); *Trendy Traditions: A Cross Cultural Skills-Based Reader of Essays*

on the United States (Macmillan Languagehouse, 2002); *Business as Usual: An Integrated Approach to Learning English* (Seibido, 2003); *Letters Home: Musings of An American Expatriate Living in Japan* (iUniverse, 2003); *Orbit: English Reading* (Sanseido, 2004); *Talking to the Other Side: A History of Modern Spiritualism and Mediumship—A Study of the Religion, Science, Philosophy and Mediums that Encompass this American-Made Religion* (iUniverse, 2005); *Orbit: English Reading* [New Edition] (Sanseido, 2007); *Talk, Talk: American-Style—Meeting People* [Book One] (Macmillan Languagehouse, 2008); and *Talk, Talk: American-Style—Going Places* [Book Two] (Macmillan Languagehouse, 2008).

Illustration and Photo Credits:

1 "Map of Aomori Prefecture," Illustration by Shigenobu Aoki, *Wikipedia Commons*, [www.wikipedia.com] Copyright Free.

2 "Koinobori, flags in the shape of koi (carp)," Photo by Fg2, *Wikipedia Commons*, [www.wikipedia.com] Copyright Free.

3 "First Japanese immigrants in Brazil, aboard Kasato Maru ship in port of Santos, Brazil," Photo circa 1908, *Wikipedia Commons*, [www.wikipedia.com] Copyright Free.

4 "Pension Handbooks of Japan," Photo by Katamakura, *Wikipedia Commons*, [www.wikipedia.com] Copyright Free.

5 "Buccinid whelks for sale at a fish market in Japan." Photo by Takahashi, *Wikipedia Commons*, [www.wikipedia.com] Copyright Free.

6 "Samurai of the Satsuma Clan during the Boshin War Period." Photo circa 1860s, *Wikipedia Commons*, [www.wikipedia.com] Copyright Free.

7 "Akebono Retirement Ceremony," Photo by Philbert Ono, *Wikipedia Commons*, [www.wikipedia.com] Copyright Free.

*All other photographs are from the author's personal collection.

